Fishing
the
Southeast Coast

D1566226

Also by Donald Millus

**A Contemplative Fishing Guide
To The Grand Strand**

Fishing
the
Southeast Coast

Essays on Fish, Fishing, Fishermen, and Fishing Places,
From Morehead City, North Carolina, Through Coastal
South Carolina, to the Georgia Sea Islands

Donald Millus

Sandlapper Publishing, Inc.
Orangeburg, South Carolina

ISBN: 0-87844-076-3 (Hardback)
ISBN: 087844-085-2 (Paperback)

Millus, Donald, 1939–
    Fishing the Southeast Coast/Donald Millus. —1st ed.
    p.   cm.
    Bibliography: p.
    Includes index.
    1. Fishing—Southern States.   2. Fishing—Atlantic
    Coast (U.S.)
I. Title.
SH464.S68M55   1989   88-30804
799.1'66148—dc19   CIP

Copyright © 1989 by Sandlapper Publishing Co., Inc.

First Edition

Manufactured in the United States of America

Portions of the text and some of the photographs in this book originally appeared in *Outdoor Life, Salt Water Sportsman*, and *South Carolina Wildlife* magazines.

Printed on non-acid paper.

Maps are by D. Bryan Stone, III.
Design work is by Linda Benefield.
Photographs are by the author, unless otherwise noted.

1 2 3 4 5 6 7 8 9 10 89 90 91 92 93 94 95 96 97 98 99

For Al and John
in memory of Dad and brother Bus,
with whom we shared never enough fishing trips

Contents

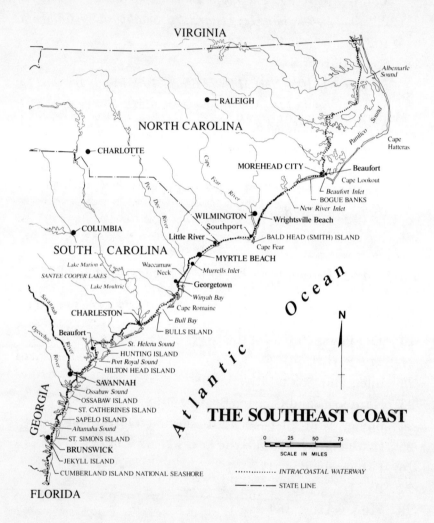

VIRGINIA

Albemarle Sound

● RALEIGH

NORTH CAROLINA

Pamlico Sound

Cape Hatteras

● CHARLOTTE

Cape Fear River

MOREHEAD CITY

Beaufort

Cape Lookout

Beaufort Inlet
BOGUE BANKS

New River Inlet

WILMINGTON

Pee Dee River

Southport

Wrightsville Beach

● COLUMBIA

Little River

BALD HEAD (SMITH) ISLAND

Cape Fear

SOUTH CAROLINA

MYRTLE BEACH

Lake Marion

Waccamaw Neck

Murrells Inlet

SANTEE COOPER LAKES

Lake Moultrie

Georgetown

Winyah Bay

Savannah River

Cape Romaine

CHARLESTON

Bull Bay

BULLS ISLAND

Ogeechee River

Beaufort

St. Helena Sound

Savannah River

HUNTING ISLAND

Port Royal Sound

HILTON HEAD ISLAND

SAVANNAH

Atlantic Ocean

GEORGIA

Ossabaw Sound

OSSABAW ISLAND

N

ST. CATHERINES ISLAND

SAPELO ISLAND

Altamaha Sound

THE SOUTHEAST COAST

ST. SIMONS ISLAND

BRUNSWICK

0   25   50   75

JEKYLL ISLAND

SCALE IN MILES

CUMBERLAND ISLAND NATIONAL SEASHORE

·············· *INTRACOASTAL WATERWAY*

——·——·—— STATE LINE

FLORIDA

Forewords

I. The Truly Dedicated Fisherman

Modern angling literature suffers from a surfeit of experts which is one of the reasons that *Fishing the Southeast Coast* is as welcome as the arrival of the season's first striped bass. Espousing no single technique and claiming no unusual skills, the author's forte is his curiosity and his seemingly boundless enthusiasm. When fishing with Don Millus, I sometimes feel rather pedestrian because I cannot match the excitement and delight he exhibits, whether he is fast to a big king mackerel or believing he has detected the nibble of a one-pound flounder.

The truly dedicated fisherman, and Don is one, immerses himself utterly in the endeavor, eschewing all thoughts of the workaday world. Such men are occasionally introduced to angling in middle life, but more often they are hooked in their formative years, as was the author of this book who caught his first fish in a pond in a New York City park while the roaring of baseball fans in a nearby stadium filled the sultry afternoon with a sound like that of the distant surf.

But, lest I have created the impression that Don thinks of nothing but fishing, I once asked him if he would be happy to be so occupied every day. His answer was no, that work—he is a professor of Medieval and Renaissance literature—came first, that each endeavor enhanced the other.

No ordinary angler and no ordinary chronicler of things piscatorial, Professor Millus is in love with the Southeast coast, and his hunger to try everything has helped him avoid that jaded condition into which long-time fishermen sometimes fall, wherein only one or two specialized forms of angling—whether it be blue water trolling for billfish or flyrodding for tarpon—continue to have appeal. He is as happy aboard a party boat, or rubbing shoulders with hordes of tourist-anglers on one of South Carolina's fishing piers, as he is with a single companion in a skiff in a choppy inlet or seining for both food and bait with his daughter in a tidal marsh. A gregarious fellow, he has a knack for locating fascinating waterfront characters and learning their secrets—such men as W.W. Hills of Charleston, South Carolina, who is better known to the angling fraternity as "Creekman." Although he lost an arm and a leg in a railroad accident, Mr. Hills loads his wheelchair and his tackle into his pickup truck and heads for the water when fish are biting.

Writers on angling who wish to appeal to as wide an audience as possible must leaven the necessary technical information with the flavor of the endeavor, with the beauty and vitality of the creature sought. To be sufficiently specific without becoming pedantic is the constant challenge, and Don Millus deals with this superbly.

He is also intensely aware of the fragility of the marine coastal environment and of the necessity to battle for its integrity, and he knows that no species of fish—no matter how fecund or wide-ranging—is safe from over-exploitation by both sporting and commercial interests. Sensitive, literate and witty, he is the embodiment of the ideal angler.

Living as I do in seacoast New England where most marine angling takes place between May and November, I sometimes envy Don's opportunity—he lives in Conway, South Carolina—to cast a line every month of the year, and I always relish his accounts of those experiences. Move with him through the seasons in the pages that follow and you'll see what I mean.

NELSON BRYANT
West Tisbury, Massachusetts

II. *Discovering the Best of the Coast*

What Lindbergh was to flying, Chaplin to comedy, and Frank Perdue to chickens, Don Millus is to that portion of the Southeast coast from North Carolina's Outer Banks to the Sea Islands of Georgia.

Over the past 15 years, he has done more to publicize local angling enterprises—from pier owners and restaurateurs to tackle dealers and charter boaters—than anyone else along the Grand Strand. But Don has done more than merely describe local conditions and personalities; he has created an awareness of Carolina's marine resources and the pleasure of fishing for them that simply did not exist in the region two decades ago.

Don speaks to and for all marine recreational anglers. Some are pier people; others prefer fishing the bays and inlets; still others explore the offshore wrecks, reefs, and blue water beyond. Don knows them all, experts and novices alike, and his thoughtful, witty byline is a tonic to countless thousands of readers of several national and regional publications.

Don's background suits him peculiarly well for the task of serving as the Grand Strand's angling amanuensis. He was a Jesuit seminarian and regent before taking a doctoral degree at Yale in English. His earlier studies help him to extract confessions—and angling secrets—from the people he interviews; his later studies provided him with a historical perspective and literary flair that distinguish his stories and articles from mere outdoor writing.

Don also served as an army officer in Vietnam, a mashed kind of experience in which he played Hawkeye Pearce to a command structure dominated by Charles Winchesters. That year fine-tuned the irony that seems to go with a birth and upbringing in Brooklyn.

Don Millus cares desperately for his adopted Carolina lowlands, and his annual labors on behalf of the world's only intercollegiate, international, and in 1985 intercontinental fishing match and seminar have caused the name of Coastal Carolina College to reverberate from the Bay of Fundy to the Sea of Japan.

Discovering the best of the Carolina coast with Don Millus has been a wonderful part of my outdoor life. Rediscovering the coast with him through these stories is even more satisfying, for so much that I missed before is now part of *Fishing the Southeast Coast.*

GEORGE REIGER
Locustville, Virginia

Preface

The Waters Are Still Alive

On a late summer afternoon my 11-year-old daughter and I are going fishing in a creek that runs into an inlet on the South Carolina coast. We had our choice of dipping blueclaw crabs with the aid of a flounder head and piece of monofilament line and a sinker, or dragging a net for shrimp, or casting one for mullet, and then going into the inlet to fish for flounder or to the jetties for bluefish or red drum. In a few weeks, we might even catch a king mackerel from our small boat. In this ecological niche that extends from near Beaufort, North Carolina, to the Georgia Sea Islands, there are hundreds of such places still left for all to enjoy.

On that particular day a few years ago, we dragged a net for shrimp and squid. My aim was bait and dinner, Sara's the gathering of a few specimens for a science project in middle school. An hour's work toward the slow-moving end of the outgoing tide produced shrimp, squid, mullet, and even a pair of fat softshelled blueclaw crabs. We used the finger-sized mullet live for bait and caught a fine puppy drum, all shining gold and copper, sporting not one but four spots near its tail. As the tide rose, we beached our boat and took a quick swim in the late-afternoon sunshine, the water clean and refreshing, our tired bodies renewed by the soothing warmth of September ocean water.

Earlier that summer my 13-year-old son and I had sailed on a headboat some 40 miles out in the Atlantic Ocean for a day of bottomfishing. Silver snapper, blueback seabass, vermilion snapper (not as big as "genuine" red or American snapper, but pretty and good to eat), and a variety of other edible bottomfeeders from the natural reef below us added to our stringer of fish in the boat's cooler. A dolphin—the beautiful fish, not the huge but graceful sea mammal—examined the tomtate I had set out on a

PREFACE

surface line for king mackerel. Later a king hit a cigar minnow drifted by another angler, and a number of four- to five-pound grouper were taken. Porpoises and flying fish put on a show, unbidden but much appreciated by the mixed crowd of tourists and local people on the full-day trip.

That fishing year was typical of any on our coast. It had started with striped bass fishing in the Intracoastal Waterway in January. I had to turn down an invitation to fish for stripers and shad in the coastal waters of Georgia in March, for the spottail bass were already enticing us to the jetties of Charleston. In the back creeks near the border between the two Carolinas, fishermen were already taking a few flounder as the temperatures climbed to the 70's in the lengthening afternoons. A friend called from near Beaufort, South Carolina, to report that big bluefish were hitting any lure trolled past them offshore, while the headboats from near Beaufort, North Carolina, were already taking out charter groups and returning with hefty stringers of snapper and grouper from the offshore reefs. Reports of cobia filtered up from Hilton Head Island in May at the same time as anglers were competing in billfish tournaments out of Georgetown, South Carolina, and preparing for them on the North Carolina coast.

Winyah Bay had been our starting point for blue water trips after yellowfin tuna and wahoo in June, while the piers of both Carolinas were seeing their late spring run of king mackerel and flounder. In early summer we used light-line slow-trolling live-bait techniques for kings, an art taught us by a Southport, North Carolina, angler. The same techniques would provide excitement and big kings in early fall, but meanwhile there were overnight trips for swordfish or for Gulf Stream bottomfishing, and the late summer run of pompano on the piers and Spanish mackerel offshore to attract us.

Off the barrier islands of North Carolina and South Carolina and Georgia, late summer would also bring fine surf fishing for big channel bass with occasional spotted sea trout as a bonus. On the piers, thousands of people who never fished until fall would take coolers full of tasty spot for the frying pan. Flounder in the inlets and trout around the jetties would take us through the fall and back to striped bass fishing in the middle of winter, whether in the Intracoastal Waterway near the North Carolina–South Carolina line or down on the Georgia coast.

Winter is the best time to take striped bass (rockfish) from
the waters of the Intracoastal Waterway and from the
rivers along the Southeast coast.

PREFACE

My children and I don't catch fish every trip out, even in good weather, but the fishing is almost always enjoyable. Twelve months a year there are fishing opportunities on our coast. The waters are still clean, the fish are still there, but it is not as it used to be. In some ways it is better, in many ways worse, but our coast still has much to offer. What has been lost elsewhere is still here to save. What follows is not only my own personal experience of our coastal fishing, but the experiences and memories of many who have fished this coast for up to half a century. In the hope that this book may make it possible for others to enjoy in the next century what we have now, and to share the experiences my family and I have had over the past dozen years, I offer my descriptions of fishing our coast. To all who have shared their experiences, their skill, their knowledge, their writings and photographs, and even their bait, tackle, boats, and secret spots with me over the past dozen years, my sincere thanks.

One could spend a vacation or a lifetime fishing the piers of the Carolina coast. Flounder, pompano, spot, saltwater trout, and king mackerel are just a few of the fish taken in season.

Part One:

The Fish

Introduction

Part of the fascination of fishing comes from the knowledge that something alive is there, just out of sight. If one just has confidence, or faith, or experience, that beautiful living creature we know as the fish may prove its presence, our knowledge, our skill, or our luck, just by biting. This is true whether one is flipping a tiny cork from a cane pole in a coastal river, throwing a plug for winter trout in an inlet, trolling a soft plastic-tailed lure for striped bass in the Intracoastal Waterway, casting a live mullet for channel bass next to a jetty, trolling a live menhaden for king mackerel just offshore, or dropping a sinker and two hooks baited with squid into the depths of the Gulf Stream. Something is alive down there.

True, there are signs that we watch for: minnows scattering as a big bass forages, mullet leaping into the air fleeing for their lives before marauding bluefish or king mackerel, birds diving over a school of baitfish whipped into a ball by hungry billfish. But usually our faith comes from experience: at this time of year, in this area, this species will be taken on this bait or lure. The great thrill of fishing is that we are at the same time surprised by the strike and we expected it all along. Perhaps fishing is a paradigm of man's faith in God, immortality, and the ultimate benevolence of the universe.

Fishermen, above all men, know death and the changes of season. To catch my dinner, both the baitfish and the predator must die. To see the beauty of a winter trout all blue and gold and green and silver and spotted, I must hook the fish and play it to my net. From out of the depths of the still and silent inlet waters, I haul against its will a beautiful fish that will become a part of me and my family, the centerpiece of a festive dinner or just some fillets fried up for lunch on an ordinary workday. But that fish becomes a part of me, rather than being eaten by a shark or dying a lonely death on some ocean shore to be dissolved, as we all will be, back into the elements of earth and sea.

18

Each fish has its own time and season and habits and wiles. Each demands that man adjust his methods of harvesting. Each has its place in the scheme of things, from toadfish to tarpon, from flying fish to flounder, from bream to blue marlin. "Glory be to God for dappled things," the poet said of trout and other creatures. The same poet, Gerard Manley Hopkins, sang the praises of the arts of man, their "tackle and trim." All the fishes of our coast, of every coast, demand the same glorification if we have eyes to see. The surprise, the beauty, and the reward of the patience, faith, and hope involved in catching some of the many game and food fish that the Southeast coast affords are not the least of our concerns here.

1

"Great abundance of . . . Spanish Mackrill"

More than 300 hundred years ago, an explorer of the Carolina coast, Robert Horne, wrote *A Brief Description of the Province of Carolina* in hopes of enkindling interest in the new world of the South Atlantic coast: "Here are as brave Rivers as any in the World, stored with great abundance of sturgeon, salmon, basse, plaice, trout, and Spanish Mackrill, with many other most pleasant sorts of Fish, both flat and round, for which the English tongue hath no name" (as quoted in "A Brief History of Commercial Fisheries in South Carolina," James M. Bishop, *Coastal Heritage*, No. 4, November–December 1982).

Horne was fabricating Carolina salmon, and Spanish mackerel rarely venture into our rivers, but like the plaice (flounder) and the sturgeon (an endangered species), Spanish mackerel are still here to delight and sometimes frustrate the summertime angler. These small mackerel do travel in huge schools, although not nearly as huge nor as abundant as they were even a decade ago, arriving in early summer and staying offshore or venturing almost into the mouths of our coastal inlets well into the autumn. Not the favorite food fish of coastal anglers, a freshly caught and iced and promptly cleaned Spanish mackerel broiled with tomatoes and onions is still a feast that neither explorer nor twentieth-century gourmet would turn down.

Like the other mackerels, Spanish often herd schools of tiny baitfish into an area and then repeatedly slash the edges of the school. Kings and bonito will sometimes be mixed in, so it pays to have some heavier leaders and tackle on hand even when the catch is mainly Spanish mackerel of two pounds or so.

An occasional 10-pounder is taken by live-bait king mackerel anglers, with the South Carolina record at one time a big Spanish taken from Springmaid Pier in Myrtle Beach on a live bait intended for a king. A wavy body line and yellow specks against its silver to blue side make the Spanish a particularly beautiful fish as it splashes out of the water holding a shiny spoon firm in its toothy jaw.

The Spanish mackerel is a fish for a leisurely summer day. The inlet fishing may slow as the waters warm and the king mackerel may move back offshore for the same reason. But armed with light tackle, spinning gear with 12-pound test line and sharpened hooks on small spoons such as the Clark or Hopkins, the angler can cruise the Atlantic, from a few hundred yards to a few miles offshore, always on the lookout for the diving birds that may signal the presence of Spanish in a feeding frenzy.

On one of those August days when the flat ocean reflects the blue sky dabbed with fat white but still unthreatening clouds, I trolled fruitlessly for king mackerel, only to have a pair of Spanish mackerel come dashing up behind our live mullet. As I watched from just a few yards away, they darted excitedly back and forth, before rejecting the baits as either too large or too clumsily rigged for their tastes. Another day, over one of our inshore artificial reefs, my son and I were fishing for flounder only to have three big fish in a row break off. They were Spanish mackerel swallowing our mullet minnows and cutting the line with their teeth. One local fisherman, frustrated by schools of Spanish mackerel that would not strike, cast live mud minnows at them and was rewarded for his innovation with a dozen fat Spanish.

The most clever method of catching Spanish mackerel I have observed is the small-gold-hook technique. A series of gold-colored hooks, brand-new and sparkling, is attached to small dropper loops on a spinning line with a small spoon as weight, and jigged alongside a pier. Small Spanish mackerel may be taken in this manner, and two or three of those will make a nice meal.

For those who do not own a boat, the charter boats of the coast will often take a party of a half-dozen anglers for a morning or afternoon of Spanish mackerel fishing at a reasonable price. The boat owner saves on fuel, not having to run far offshore to find the Spanish, and on bait, for the Clark spoon is by far the most effective bait summer in and summer out.

Our inshore reefs are proven attractors for Spanish mackerel. Early morning is usually the best time to fish. Late afternoon on fair summer days just off the beaches may also be a good time to catch these mackerel in a feeding mood. Whatever the time or occasion, use light tackle and have a cooler ready to ice down a tasty dinner. These small gamefish can make a day on the coastal waters of Georgia and the Carolinas a most pleasant memory.

2

The Flounder, Laziest of Fish

Hold one hand in front of you and tap the back of it smartly with the index finger of your other hand. That's all the bite you will feel as you troll a mud minnow in a coastal inlet or tidal river or next to a jetty in quest of one of the most delicious bottomfishes and, yes, gamefishes, too, of the Southeast coast. But when you feel that tap, let the flounder swallow that fat live minnow. Give it time to slowly engulf the baitfish with its oversized mouth. Allow the flounder to swallow it down to his anal spot, for neither it nor you should be in a hurry. Count to at least 30 and you will rarely lose a flounder. Now strike.

While you are anticipating the feel of a flounder on a light but stiff six-foot baitcasting or spinning rod, let me tell you one of Mr. Rudy's favorite flounder stories. It has to do with the flounder's awesome maw and hungry nature. (No doubt Gunter Grass's literary flounder would protest over the manners of his New World cousins.) It seems that Mr. Rudy, retired from service in the U.S. Air Force, was fishing from a coastal pier and caught a six-inch whiting. Knowing that some three- to four-pound flounder had been caught recently (it was the month of June, a time of especial hope for aficionados of our Southern flounder), he put a flounder hook in the tail of the whiting and dropped it down to swim around near the bottom next to the pier. A half-hour later he checked his bait, only to discover that a flounder hardly ten inches long had managed to make a whiting sandwich of the live bait and had swallowed the whole thing, a fish just slightly shorter than itself.

Such are the appetites of our flounder, whose two eyes on the top side of their bodies are not bigger than their stomachs, but are the information processors for enormous appetites. Perhaps there is some flounder in each of us. After all, the flounder is designed to lie in wait on the bottom, its body camouflaged and taking on the coloration of its surroundings—light for sand, darker for mud—and its two eyes watching for unwary baitfish, targets of opportunity.

"Flounder are mainly sight feeders," I am reminded on our annual fishing trips by flounder expert George Reiger of *Field & Stream* magazine. But Reiger also knows that flounder are unpredictable. One fall afternoon he announced magisterially that fishing was over for the day, although I think he preferred to meditate on the melancholy aspects of a broken graphite rod and a lost chance to tag and release a 15-pound spottail bass that he had fought dramatically for 10 minutes on ultralight tackle before an appreciative audience of two. But there was too much of the ebb tide left next to a coastal jetty for me to quit. Before I picked up my spinning rod with plastic-tailed grub to cast for one last red drum, I baited a rod with a live mullet minnow and placed it next to the now napping author.

It was a good thing that I had placed the flounder rod in a holder, for as our anchored boat swayed away from the rocks on a swell, the rod took on a deep bend and the reel sang out. Even a sleepy outdoor writer can sense the difference between a hang-up and a fish-on, and before I could set my own rod down, Reiger had eagerly snatched the bending rod from the holder and set the hook. The fish did not run, a sure sign it was neither spottail nor saltwater trout, and its throbbing reluctance to come out of the depths was encouraging: the slower they come up, the bigger they are. It was indeed a flounder, some five pounds, and at its own leisurely pace it had swallowed the live mullet bait. Even a dormant angler can be successful with flounder.

But while indolence is sometimes rewarded, the diligent flounder fisherman works hard at his task of the day. Live bait is essential for serious flounder fishing, so flounder experts such as Roy Brigham plan their day of flounder fishing on the Carolina coast with care. Live mud minnows must be trapped the day before or early in the morning, the fatter the better. When finger mullet are available, a net must be thrown in a creek or swash to

Late spring and summer finds anglers drifting for flounder in the inlets of the Carolinas and Georgia, but flounder ("fluke" to Northerners) may also be taken through the fall months.

ensure a good supply of mullet baits for pier fishing for flounder. But whether one fishes from a pier, or in a creek or river along the Southeast coast, the flounder fisherman is always on the alert for that much-anticipated tap that tells him that something is there.

How does one find that hole by the jetties or in the inlet or coastal river that will produce flounder? Trial and error, observation, perhaps even the generosity of a confirmed flounder angler. But if someone is so kind as to show you his favorite flounder hole, don't be so ungrateful as to bring a bunch of your friends there the next day. Show some respect.

Slow trolling or drifting is the key to presenting that frisky mud minnow or finger mullet. Sharpen that flounder hook, hook the baitfish gently through both lips, use as light a weight as possible on the three-way rigs available at any coastal tackle shop in the Carolinas or Georgia. Give that hook fresh from the tackle shop an extra sharpening with your hookstone. Then troll it slowly. No more than a 15-horsepower motor is used by most local flounder specialists. (The Johnson 15 is a particular favorite because of its rugged ability to slow troll for years in the salty environment of our coast.) Your boat should be small, of shallow draft, and loaded with rod holders and those yellow plastic flow-through bait buckets essential to keeping your minnows alive and well.

With your motor at slow troll, or as you cut the motor and drift, the important sounds of the coast are more easily heard. Kingfishers and oyster catchers are the background music, but the occasional splash of a big mullet or the scattering of a school of mullet or shrimp before the well-named "snapper" blues are also part of the symphony. Wading birds, the ripple of the wind in the spartina grass, and the movement of current around and across an oyster bar are just part of the visual background of trolling for flounder. But always there is that intense concentration required on the rod in hand, that waiting for the tap that is different from an oyster shell or the nasty grabbing of a bait by a mean blueclaw crab. More than one blind fisherman has developed a reputation as a superior flounder angler, outfishing sighted companions by sheer sensitivity of touch.

If you stay with it, the tapping bites will come. The longer you fish for flounder, and the more you learn the right combinations of season, tides, productive locations, and live baits artfully presented, the more flounder will be hooked by your patient strike. You will feel that potential mouth-watering dinner putting its flat, thick body sideways to the pull of your rod. Gently now, ease that fat flatfish toward the waiting net, wielded by yourself, or, ideally, by a companion who can appreciate the gentle sounds and the soft sights of a day of flounder fishing on a coastal river or inlet.

For those who don't own a boat, there are a few marinas along our coasts within reach of good flounder holes. There you can rent a small boat and motor for a day of flounder fishing. For those who prefer to fish for flounder from dry land, or at least not in a boat, the piers and some of the jetties provide many opportunities. Live mullet or mud minnows may be cast back under the piers or if the hour is early and the pier uncrowded one can even "troll" a live bait by slowly walking along and moving it from piling to piling in hope of that encouraging tap. Many of the piers have drop nets that should be used when a flounder of more than a pound is hooked. The odds of losing a flounder flipping at the end of a line are good if one tries to hoist it into a boat or up on a pier without the aid of a landing net.

From the jetties, flounder fishing is not as convenient because of the difficulties of sliding a flounder up on the slippery rocks, but a long-handled net and experienced anglers can do the job, albeit very carefully. Remember that dry-looking rocks can be very slippery. Needless to say, I do most of my flounder fishing from a boat, for I like to have the sights and sounds of flounder fishing to myself, or, at most, share them with one good fishing companion.

Flounder, despite their deliberate feeding habits and slow-moving lifestyle, are surprising fish. One overcast fall day I cast a lure for spotted sea trout from a bank next to some spot fishermen only to have a five-pound flounder stop the lure dead in its tracks in a foot of water. I assumed I had been hung up, but when the hang-up moved and throbbed I had a thrashing flounder to slide up before an unappreciative audience. Having fished all day for a few spot, they found my luck intolerable and gave up fishing for the day.

Professor Donald Kelly of Francis Marion College in Florence, South Carolina, is a devotee of flounder fishing on the North

oast, but one of his most memorable flounders came
friendly intercollegiate competition at the jetty at
Beach State Park in South Carolina. While others
luefish, he tipped a plastic grub with a bit of shrimp
and promptly nailed a four-pound flatfish. Grubs tipped with
live mullet or mud minnows will often induce flounder strikes
when the fish are apparently not hungry. Illinois angler Tom
Owens swears that spinners mounted above a flounder hook
produce more Carolina flounder for him. No one argues with a
successful angler, particularly if he is filleting a stringer of thick
flounder or carefully preparing one to be stuffed with sauteed
shrimp or crabmeat. The best thing about flounder fishing may
still be the pleasure they provide at table. Even better is the
flounder as *piece de resistance* for a supper which you have caught
yourself from our coastal waters.

3

Eight Kings A-Leaping

A strong wind was blowing steadily from the east. Not even
the most hopeful angler could expect it to ease off before night.
An offshore trip was a distinctly uncomfortable prospect, but
inside the inlet huge schools of mullet were leaping in the autumn
air, "cloudy bright" as the directions included with 35mm film
would have it, a marginal day, at least in its first impressions, for
the pursuit of king mackerel. But one learns to be surprised by
the sea and its creatures, even after decades of fishing. "The
longer you fish, the more you find you don't know," was the way
an old fisherman on a Cape Ann, Nova Scotia, lobster boat once
put it to me.

Between the push of the wind and the pull of the moon, the
tide was high and still flooding in. Falling water that would herd
the mullet within easy range of a net cast from the beach was
still three hours away. The first battle of the day for a king
mackerel angler is often just catching bait.

Anyone who has fished south of Cape Hatteras knows that the
king mackerel is the saltwater equivalent of a baseball triple crown

winner: the king has size and power that make for spectacular strikes, especially when it can be induced to hit a lure at the surface or, even better, a slowly trolled live baitfish; this smashing, crashing, surprising strike would be the angling equivalent of the home run. Although their numbers have declined drastically in the past decade—so badly, in fact, that limits have been imposed on catches, first off Florida and later along the whole Atlantic Coast—one can usually count on catching more than a few kings on a good trip; thus the king is the r.b.i. leader for many a charter fleet south of Cape Hatteras. The king is not a shy feeder either, with trollers ranging from a few miles offshore to out near the Gulf Stream depending on the kings for most of their gamefish hits from early spring until late in the fall. The king is the hit man one can count on off the Georgia and Carolina coasts, the Pete Rose of angling on our coast in the '60s, '70s, and even in the angling decline of the '80s.

By the end of September (I am writing this just as the waters are beginning to cool at the end of a hot summer) a number of

King mackerel hang around the artificial reefs of the Carolina and Georgia coast. This one hit a live pinfish and ran around the marker buoy (background) before the author's son, Donnie, brought it to the gaff.

25- to 35-pound kings will be caught off Myrtle Beach area piers, while anglers in tournaments in Southport and Wrightsville Beach, North Carolina, may well be weighing in some 40 pounders within the next four weeks. By the end of the month sport fishermen from Little River, Murrells Inlet, and Georgetown will have wound up a three-day quest for the biggest and heaviest kings in the Arthur Smith tournament, while fishermen out of Charleston, Hilton Head, and Edisto Island will be looking forward to their fall weekends because of the kings. Down off Savannah, Professor Paul Ward and his fellow faculty fishing enthusiasts at Armstrong State will be anticipating catching the biggest kings of the year over the artificial reefs and wrecks that lie 20 miles or more off the Georgia coast. Even headboat anglers fishing for black sea bass will be able to take kings on live-lined baitfish.

Especially in the fall, the king mackerel is still THE gamefish that offshore, inshore, and pier fishermen count on. Rarely do kings run under 8 pounds, while torpedolike monsters of 40 pounds and more thrill anglers every year. But even a 10- to 20-pound king, a size not unusual even for pier fishermen or for anglers slowly trolling live mullet, bluefish, or menhaden from a 14-foot boat just outside our inlets, is an impressive fish. The king's toothy jaws that can slice a rigged mullet in half, often just a whisker behind the hook, combined with its speed and savage strike, make it one of angling's last encounters with a kind of primitive energy that borders on the awesome. Nature seems to have designed the king as a terrorist: fast, powerful, cunning, with eyesight so sharp that it can spot just where a hook is in a trolled ballyhoo and slice off a third of the baitfish without touching a hook. Combine a leaping ability that will take it to the eye level of a skipper sitting on a flying bridge—Captain Owen Daly testifies to this—and the ability to run repeatedly even after an angler is sure he has whipped a king, and its appeal to both new and experienced anglers is quite understandable.

Captain Owen Daly, a retired U.S. Army colonel, was reflecting on the king mackerel as we prepared to sail one fine May day from South Carolina's Georgetown Landing Marina near the head of Winyah Bay: "When I first began to run a charter boat back in the fifties, it was no trick to drag a few spoons for kings and fill the fish box by eleven. Now you have to work hard to get them."

If the kings are getting more scarce, they are still around, some days with enough to fill at least a small fish box by early afternoon. As a friend and I prospected for mullet on that blustery fall day a few years ago, my hopes were not soaring. Still, I managed to luck into a one-pound mullet as I threw a cast net blindly on the Huntington Beach side of Murrells Inlet.

More experienced anglers with bigger nets will take dozens of menhaden and keep them alive in specially designed and aerated live-bait tanks on their boats, but we were content to put our precious solitary mullet in my rusty old Coleman cooler with a wood frame and screen replacing a battered top that had long ago been discarded. The plastic inside of the cooler, complete with drain plug essential for changing the water frequently, still made for a fine live-bait tank of generous proportions fitting the ideal half-pound live mullet so suited to slow trolling for kings. (More elaborately equipped boats have bait tanks—barrels with through-the-hull aeration suited to carrying hundreds of live menhaden to offshore fishing grounds. Inshore, my old cooler or a minnow trolling bucket can do quite nicely if catching fish is not a matter of life or death or thousands of dollars.) We headed for the ocean to troll our one beautiful baitfish, fat with dark stripes, an unwilling conspirator in our quest for a king.

The fish hung there suspended before us. It looked to be at least six feet long and over 50 pounds, but the extra length and weight in my first estimate were no doubt due to the chemical reactions induced in my system by its sudden appearance in the air, accompanied by the water coming together where it had fractured the surface of the inlet. I had been looking out toward the ocean. A charter boat was trolling slowly along between the jetties, and I wondered why the captain was fishing there. I didn't see the start of the leap of the king scarcely 10 yards ahead of our small boat. (It is an old but useful vessel, a Grumman vee-hull which does quite nicely in seas up to four feet or so, and that, in still warm weather with other boats around to rely on in the unlikely case of trouble, would allow us to venture a few hundred yards even into a fairly rough ocean.)

At a cost of some 22 million dollars, the U.S. Army Corps of Engineers constructed these jetties to enable fishing boats, commercial and sport, and other pleasure craft to have easy access to the inlet. Incidentally, the jetties provide great fishing, for they are the equivalent of artificial reefs, not only sheltering fish but sheltering fishermen and their boats in rough weather. Imagine a funnel, with the wider trough seen in outline from above, a "Y" with its bottom split apart to allow a sheltered straightaway coming in from the ocean, opening up into a wider bay fully protected from the south winds, with a weir to the north that is underwater only at flood tide. Running from the Garden City shore on the north side of Murrells Inlet and from the Huntington Beach side to the south, the rocks, lower to allow for the movement of sand on the north side, black-topped and ideal for walking on the south, converge before the last few hundred yards of straightaway leading to the ocean. On that windy day in October, the king mackerel had surged in with tide and wind, even beyond the straightaway. Now they were leaping around our boat.

My companion, Mike Schroder, is a golf professional of cool nerves who has competed with the best of the Tour players and bested many of them many times. Calmly he asked me whether the kings jumped like this often. "No," I shouted, not even considering any attempt to hide my excitement. "This is the first time in seven years of fishing these jetties that I've seen this happen." I did admit that I had expected it to happen someday ("expect" in the true Latin sense of the word, "to hope") given the right conditions of kings, baitfish, tide, and wind, but that it should occur on my friend's first fishing trip strained coincidence. "It's unfair," I yelled above the wind and chugging motor, but it was funny: My chances of breaking 100 on my first golf outing were nil, while an inexperienced fisherman should on his first trip have a chance at a trophy king. On second thought, I know that such chance is one of the things that makes fishing an attractive sport, pastime, recreation, and even occupation.

By the time we had trolled past the tip of the south jetty, Schroder had counted eight kings leaping in the inlet behind and in front of us. On the jetty, people calmly fished for croakers and spottail, but I only had eyes for the waves surging into the mouth of the inlet. My ears, however, strained against the wind for a sound that was not long in breaking out, the sound of the ocean opening suddenly and violently as another king broke the surface. I turned and my eyes caught the fish in midair. Its crash back into the dark water was followed instantly by the racket of a reel screeching as our mullet headed out to sea firmly in the jaws of a king. I handed the rod to my golf teacher, with line still peeling off the reel as the king headed into the center of the rough water flooding into the inlet.

Schroder was into the first king of his life, a fish 25 times the size of any he had ever hooked in saltwater and with far more ability to run and fight than any fish of comparable size he could ever hook in freshwater. He was using a one-piece graphite rod with a very light tip, his line was no more than 20-pound test, and the drag was set very lightly lest the tiny treble trailer hooks pull out, a distinct possibility with heavier tackle. "I can't believe how this fish is pulling," was his first response, the sentiments of many a first-time king fisherman.

Another boat was headed out of the inlet, a Boston Whaler trolling what looked like popping plugs in an attempt to interest the fish that its crew observed jumping all around us. The charter boat, still fishless, for it was dragging lures suited to kings in deep water, had veered off when the skipper saw our hookup, but the Whaler was heading for my guest's fish, which by now had taken over a hundred yards of line against a lightly set drag. I yelled, I screamed, I shouted, and I waved, all to no avail. But by some special grace, perhaps reserved for the first-timer with his premier king, the fish did not get hung up on the other boat nor on its lines. Of course, the swells at the mouth of the inlet may have induced our neighbors to turn aside from their sea-going direction. Whatever, Schroder started moving line back on his reel, as I kept the bow headed into the swells.

"Pump the rod gently back and reel on the way down; guide the line onto the reel so it doesn't bunch up; keep the pressure on him; don't reel too fast; don't jerk the rod suddenly." A captain always gives enough directions so that if a fish is lost, the poor neophyte angler knows whose fault it is. Besides, this is the revenge of the high handicapper for all those "you came off the ball's" or "you raised up's" or "your hands were too floppy's."

Slowly, but not inevitably for that would spoil the suspense, my companion worked the fish toward the boat. Four times the king surged away from us and the reel's drag allowed line to give and not break. Each time the fish saw the boat, it dived, twice attempting to go under the boat. By keeping the motor in gear and turning away from the fish we avoided trouble. It was my turn to be the pro, but as I sank the gaff and carefully hoisted the king over the side, I felt the weakness in the limbs that is the occasional companion of angling fulfillment. Any experienced sport fisherman knows that there is a feeling of accomplishment in letting your guest do the honors on the first fish, especially if it represents a first angling conquest.

We put another king in the boat later that day, but only after the tide fell and we were able to net some more live mullet. I lost another big one that hit a live mullet not once but twice. Our two fish, total weight just about 50 pounds, had to be cut in half to fit into our cooler, so there really was no more room for the last king of the day. Unlike a traditional charter trolling trip using heavy tackle for mackerel, live-line, light tackle trolling turns a strike into an adventure and one fish into an angling triumph.

There are times when only traditional trolling will do and some of these are memorable. There was the day when the students in our annual intercollegiate fishing match and seminar, the Coastal Carolina Invitational, tagged 54 kings over the Ten Mile Reef. There was that one special king that soared into the air at the end of a local pier, a bluefish that had just been knocked free from an angler's hook secure in the jaws of the soaring king, the angler looking on with his eyes filling with tears. There were those four kings that hit at once on an offshore November troll, and the summertime kings that were hitting drifted cigar minnows just outside the Charleston jetties, while trollers ploughed the offshore waters in vain. There were those October mornings, first boat on the artificial reef off Georgia's sunny coast, when the kings seemed never to tire of slashing at anything dragged before them or those tournament days off the North Carolina coast when it seemed that all the smaller kings in the world wanted to make deadly passionate love to our baits.

Every king angler has his or her favorite story. This fish is of the stuff that legends are made on. If we run out of kings along our coast, much of the excitement of inshore and offshore fishing will be lost forever.

P.S. That early September trip I mentioned above produced my first king of the fall. The next day my son and I took one of his young friends, Matt Ambrosino, with us and Matt put his maiden king in the boat, a 12-pounder laden with roe. Life sometimes follows art or it's easier to write about king mackerel when one has a touch of the fever. Tomorrow, the second Wednesday of September, I hope the seas will again be flat, the mullet plentiful, and the kings inshore and hungry.

P.P.S. Editing the above just before Christmas, I fondly recall the rainy, windy October morning of the autumn just finished when Tom Wiemken and I took five kings weighing, in total, just over 130 pounds, right in the mouth of the inlet. But more of that another time.

4

Everybody's Favorite Cobia Story

Saltwater anglers who have fished the Carolina and Georgia coast for a long time all have their favorite cobia stories, whether they have caught one or not. To catch a cobia requires skill and luck, and this leaves most of us cobia-less most of the time. "Your cobia is not your everyday fish" someone may be thinking; "nor mine" I might add. I have fished for cobia on numerous occasions, hooked a few, and boated one. Putting a cobia in the boat, however, does not mean that you have caught the fish. And thereon hangs many a cobia fishing tale, for this fish is a critter that is in a class by itself.

Imagine a far-smarter-than-average fish that is built somewhat like a catfish, more wide than deep, with powerful shoulders, a seemingly perpetual curiosity, and the ability to wreck a boat and terrorize its occupants. The cobia has a stripe on its side, not to indicate its racing ability, for it is more dogged than fast, but as a sign of its love of battle, a mark that usually becomes more scarred with age.

A comparison may help the reader who has not met a cobia. At the Santee-Cooper lakes in the midlands of South Carolina, hundreds of 40-pound-plus catfish will be caught in deep water each year. The angler sets the hook with lines of 20 to 40 pounds, feels the rod bend and the fish surge off, and begins pumping the fish to the surface. On the way up, the catfish will take line a few times. On the surface it may surge away, but usually it is netted, dumped on the floor of the boat, and then, carefully, to avoid its spines, put in the fish box for show and tell and fillets. Avoid the spines and the jaws and you have dinner for 10. Now imagine a fish the size of that catfish that can swim four times as fast, jump, inspect and reject baits with the cold disdain of a pampered Siamese, and then knock out boat seats, smash rods and coolers, and even send tackle boxes and gas tanks flying, to say nothing of influencing brave men to jump out of a boat into which a still "green" (read "not-yet-whipped") cobia has been presumptuously and untimely brought.

Beaufort's Jack Skinner has probably caught more cobia than any other fisherman in the Carolinas. This is his description of a typical cobia fight: "First thing the cobia does is head for the bottom, one good run, then come to the boat. You want to hold the roe (female) in the water—she's the biggest fish—the buck will get excited. The male gets frantic and he will hit whatever bait you throw at him. But make sure when you get them in the boat you have a hammer handy."

W.W. Hills, better known to Charlestonians as Creekman, tells what many consider to be the best cobia story of all. Now Creekman is himself a battler, surviving the amputation of an arm and a leg by a railroad train he had been working on. Over the past decade he has been one of the most popular speakers on our coast, for he is not only an expert raconteur but a fisherman who season-in, season-out, will catch flounder, stripers, trout, sheepshead, and more when others are complaining about tides and weather. Creekman hops out of his pickup, unloads his wheelchair, guides it to the dock, and gets in his boat for a day of fishing, often followed around by anglers envious of his hard-earned knowledge of the waters of Charleston Harbor and its tributary Low Country rivers.

It seems, Creekman relates, that he and a friend were doing some sheepshead fishing one day from one of our coastal jetties. Two guys come by in a boat, and all of a sudden one is pointing frantically into the water near a channel marker. The both of them get very excited, they circle their boat, and throw a lure near the marker where it disappears in a mighty rush of water and fish mouth. They have hooked a big cobia. The cobia pays little attention to the hooks in its jaw, but comes up to the boat gently, perhaps out of curiosity. One of the anglers opportunistically gaffs the cobia, a fish of some 40 to 50 pounds and heaves it in the boat.

The gospel according to Creekman continues: First the cobia busts four rods, then two boat seats, and then knocks a big tackle box out of the boat. By this time both fishermen have backed up on the bow and one is pointing his revolver at the fish. (Some Low Country fishermen carry revolvers when they fish to dispatch snakes, sharks, rays, and other creatures they consider dangerous.) The angler takes aim at the cobia before his friend realizes what he is about to do and yells about a wooden boat and a gas tank. Reason finally prevails. The cobia is allowed to jump out of the boat, leaving our anglers in peace and their boat and tackle in pieces.

Then there's the story of the anglers who abandoned their small wooden boat for a mudflat when a river cobia, again boated green, began its revenge. George Reiger tells the story of a cobia taken off the northern part of our coasts that repeatedly raised the cover of a cooler even though a 200-pound man was sitting on it. Fish boxes wrecked by cobia are a dollar a dozen, even with inflation. One scientific book, *Fishes of the Gulf of Mexico*, by H. Dickson Hoese and Richard H. Moore, comments that "the cobia shows little relationship to any other living fish." Anyone who has ever encountered a cobia firsthand will appreciate the fine irony in the good doctors' pronouncement, for this fish is truly in a class by itself.

Nor is the cobia's capacity for battle in the water less considerable. *New York Times* outdoor writer Nelson Bryant relates the story of a cobia hooked by Tommy Dosher of Bald Head Island, North Carolina, that took almost a half-hour in getting to the boat. Creekman insists that the toughest fish he ever fought was a two-pound cobia on six-pound test line in Charleston Harbor.

Ray Scribner, who runs charter trips from South Carolina's Fripp Island, tells of the cobia that hit a "Cisco Kid" lure one day when he was fishing with Marine Corps marksman Jack Ward. Seems that Ward went to put a hole in the cobia's head with a .38 and managed to put a hole precisely down the length of the big lure. He then gaffed the fish, tossed it up in the air into the boat, and when the fish came off the gaff he took another swipe at it and missed. "Fortunately," relates Scribner, "the fish fell in the boat, the treble hooks from the freshly cored lure didn't penetrate my leg past the barb, and the belly wound I got from the gaff was only superficial." Cobia will do that to you.

My two favorite cobia are the one at the Murrells Inlet bell buoy that grabbed my live eel, swam around my boat, looked me right in the eye, tossed its head right, then left, and then threw the eel and hook back at me, and the one I caught yesterday. Yesterday was a September day that started out hot and foggy and ended up with a spectacular lightning *cum* hail-and-rain display that rolled down from the North Carolina beaches. In the middle of the day I was trolling for king mackerel with live one-pound mullet when I noticed a two-foot cobia molesting my baits. With my spinning rod, I threw him a live mullet which he promptly swallowed. He then swam under my boat, no doubt planning to take a nap in the shade I had provided to go with the lunch I had also provided.

I pulled on the little graphite rod, but to the cobia that seemed just a token annoyance. Finally, when he realized I was too rude to take a hint, he dived for the bottom and only after five minutes with rod and net did I manage to put him in the boat. He lay there, first having spit out, disdainfully, of course, my flounder hook. (Try spitting out a flounder hook so curved that it should be unspittable; cobia cover that subject in kindergarten, no doubt.) Despite his small size, he already had some scars on his side and top. Had he picked a fight with a boat propeller or a shark? Had he, despite his tender years, already wrecked some-one's new light tackle outfit? As he lay there in the boat at my mercy, it seemed he was gesturing with his fins. I took a rag and carefully laid hold of him behind his head. What could I do but release him, in the hope that he would grow to add to the cobia legend?

Cobia Notes: Live eels, menhaden, mullet, pretty much any live baits, as well as halves of softshell blueclaw crab are favorite items in the cobia diet. Check out the buoys off the southern reaches of our coast beginning in late spring. Cobia will move from the offshore wrecks and reefs into the rivers and into the surf off our piers as the season progresses. Gulf Stream headboat anglers will hook cobia on live lines, but whether fishing for a cobia 60 miles out or at the mouth of a coastal inlet or bay, it pays to drift your bait well away from the boat. Besides being curious, cobia are by nature suspicious. Stout tackle is no guarantee that you will catch a cobia, even if you hook one. Whatever you do with a cobia, do it very carefully.

5

Bluefish Are Really Good to Eat, Too

The early morning fog had dissipated as we slipped past the sea buoy and the sun was shining on an ocean of one- to two-foot waves and the prospects of the first offshore day of early spring. Like most anglers on the Carolina or Georgia coast enjoying the warmth and anticipation of that first trip of the new fishing year, our hearts were set on king mackerel. What the sea takes away (or fails to deliver) it sometimes gives back or "what's the commotion over there?" as we cruise the Atlantic 20 miles out.

Bluefish is often the tackle-straining and fishbox-filling answer to that question off the Southeast coast in the spring as huge schools of these predators, sometimes 20 pounds or more and rarely under 10 pounds, make their way to their summer feeding grounds off New Jersey, New York, and New England. But while they are passing through, they make for exciting fishing. The bottom line with bluefish is that they are easy to catch and put up an acrobatic fight if you don't overmatch them with tuna-sized tackle or deep planers and other hardware.

Despite our nefarious intentions toward the kings—from the fishes' point of view, that is—we were also ready for the blues. After a few of our Sea Witches with mullet strip had been massacred and the attackers identified as 30 pounds worth of two fighting bluefish still snapping in the fish box, we unhooked the spinning outfits, eight-foot one-piece rods with long handles to make casting easy, and flipped surface plugs with wire leaders to the edge of the feeding fish.

First you see the splash that engulfs your lure and then hardly a second later you feel the solid hit as your plug disappears and your reel gets its first test of the year. The blue will make one fast run, not terribly long, and then it may make a few jumps. Depending on how light your line is and how you play the fish,

Sportsmen such as George Reiger appreciate not only the good fight put up by a bluefish, but the tablefare the early-season blues provide, baked or broiled.

it may take from 5 to 15 minutes to put a light tackle blue in the boat. Your wrist will be telling you to rest a minute before getting into another one, but your adrenaline and other chemical indicators will be appealing to something primitive that says "get back in there and fight." Whether you wait or charge back with another cast, the school of blues will still be there chasing that bait and your lures. Another nice thing about the early-season blues is that they do not spook easily.

As the season moves on, the blues will move in over wrecks to within a few miles of the coast and some big ones will be hung by live-bait anglers fishing for kings from our coastal piers. A few will even give surfcasters a thrill, but not in the huge numbers that Cape Hatteras and more northern beaches sometimes provide.

Headboat anglers will also catch some big blues. One headboat fisherman gutted a potential state record a few years back, much to the dismay of the owners of the boat who always welcome a little extra publicity. But the gutting of a big blue brings up another question: "Does anyone eat bluefish?" To someone from Louisiana or Cape Cod, the question is absurd. Cajuns and Cape Codders both know what a delicacy the bluefish is baked and stuffed or broiled with any number of vegetable and sauce combinations. But fry a bluefish in deep fat the way you cook bream and other flatfish and you have ruined a fish fit for a gourmet. A word to the wise is all you get here, *verb. sap. sat.*, as my high school civics teacher, Cy Egan, used to put it.

Now that we are picking at the bones of our stuffed and baked big bluefish, let's be practical and catch a mess of our more typical blues, the one-half to three pounders that are sometimes available well into the winter and then again in early spring from our piers, surf, and inlets. These are the fish that save trips when the trout and red drum are scarce, or at least make sure that the plastic-tailed lures you fish for trout are fished extra slow. Speed up a retrieve and bam, pull, splash, a blue is trying to bend your casting rod in half. Flip him in the boat—better keep some small wire leaders handy in case lures are being cut off—get them on the ice right away and split and cleaned as soon as you get back to shore; bake or broil them up fresh that night or the next day at the latest and you won't mind the inconvenience of the saltwater trout being off their feed one day.

Fish any of our beaches from North Carolina through Georgia in the early fall and expect more of the same, sometimes two blues at a time on those double hook rigs with either heavy monofilament or light wire to protect against the teeth. The last three hours of incoming tide and the first hour of the outgoing are usually best, but blues will hit at any time or on any tide if they are so inclined.

Jigged Hopkins or Mannolure lures, Bingo or Mirrolure plugs, and any of the bucktails such as the Floreo with artificial hair will do fine. A small wire leader is a good idea, unless the blues are particularly picky which is rarely the case. Fresh-cut mullet is the best bet for bait, but whole live mullet work wonders if you have them. Normally the baby blues are such voracious feeders that a small hunk of fresh mullet will do the job—quickly.

Make sure that you have a cooler with plenty of ice to protect the flavor of the freshly caught bluefish. And even if the blues ruin a few of your mud minnows trolled for flounder, don't curse at them and break their necks as I have seen some anglers do. If you don't want to eat him, release him and learn to move your flounder bait more gently and not stir up the ire of the irascible bluefish. When nothing else is available, the bluefish may provide a lot of sport besides being a treat for those who have good taste in seafood and know how to prepare it.

Blue Notes: Be careful handling them, for bluefish have sharp teeth and the bigger ones can mangle a finger or worse. On a larger scale, be aware that overfishing of bluefish stocks may make their abundance a thing of the past. They are pelagic and they are cyclical, so even without help from man, bluefish may become scarce as they were earlier this century. Even with a good thing like the blue, management is needed. As a special bonus for reading this far, keep in mind that a live one-pound bluefish is the ideal bait for float fishing or drifting for big king mackerel, spring or fall. Ask a Georgia boy like Charles Putney Johnson about that or just talk to the king fishermen on any coastal pier.

6

Man Versus Shark

A piano-sized swirl in the still morning water on the ocean side of the jetty was followed by the rapid alarum of a reel with line running out on a freespool. The click was on not only to warn us but to keep the line from tangling when the inevitable strike came. On the pier that rapid-fire click can waken sleeping king mackerel anglers; in the boat it's just like a shot of adrenaline. We were not fishing for records but for fun, so I handed the rod to John Davis, who was on his Labor Day holiday from editing *South Carolina Wildlife*. The click was not fast enough to indicate that a king mackerel had grabbed the one-pound whiting we had on for bait. I was fairly sure that it was a shark, and I hoped that it would have "shoulders," wallop enough, that is, to give our freshwater fisherman a suitable introduction to small-boat big-game fishing on our Southeast coast.

"Brace yourself and flip that lever forward, John." He put the reel into gear and the rod bent toward the water, almost pulling him off his feet. To tell the truth, the noise he uttered was probably akin to the grunt of someone punched in the stomach. Because Davis was standing near the bow of my little aluminum boat, the force of the strike pivoted the boat toward the shark which was now taking the line against a rather strongly set drag.

My guest, despite my gentle warnings, had not been completely convinced of the power that a shark packs, even one that was hardly more than 75 pounds. (Of course, this was an estimate, for we had all the fillets we wanted from the spottail and flounder taken on the dawn change of tide. We cut the line after Davis had battled the shark to boatside.) Henry David Thoreau once said that "the most populous and civilized city cannot scare a shark from its wharves." He was commenting on the wilderness that is the ocean. It is an ocean that still has huge sharks for the average fisherman to encounter—very carefully—all along the Carolina and Georgia coasts.

Whether one is using spinning tackle and taking 4- to 15-pound dogfish and hammerheads, trolling with medium tackle and enjoying the leaps of spinners and blacktips that will sock a slowly trolled mullet at an inlet mouth, or baiting with half a Spanish mackerel and using marlin-sized big-game tackle for tigers that have run, at least in one notable instance, to a ton in size (see Chapter 16, "Big-Game Fishing's Greatest Catch"), shark fishing along the Southeast coast provides he-man and super-woman sport from spring through late fall. Bays, inlets, surf, and almost anyplace in the ocean, including inlets and sounds, may have visiting sharks looking for a meal.

For those who want to tackle sharks in the 100-pound class and up, it might be a good idea to go out at least once with an experienced shark fisherman and observe carefully. They are sometimes too tough for one person to handle. A late summer shark I once encountered is a good example.

It was the day between registration at Coastal Carolina College and the first day of class and the air and ocean were too inviting to be ignored. The assistant professor asked his patient spouse to pack a lunch for him, and he trailered his boat to the inlet and ran it out past the jetties to drift a half-mile off shore. Whiting, spot, and trout were hitting small cut baits, and there would be enough fillets for a few meals. Hoping to catch a king mackerel, he had hooked a live spot on a wire leader. His reel was one of those old Ocean City bay jobs with a gear lever that flipped away from the side plate, like an ironing board coming out of a wall closet. The 1/0 reel was loaded with 20-pound test monofilament line.

As he sat back to enjoy a ham sandwich and savor the last vacation day before the term, our academic type noticed a bird hovering over his bait. The tern started to dive, he yelled to scare it—who wants to hook a bird?—and the ocean erupted in a huge swirl of gray, to pink, to white and foam. No king mackerel but a shark was on, and the five-foot rod and smallish reel seemed a bit overmatched.

The professor, however, was in no hurry and the shark was determined to take the boat for a ride. The small aluminum boat, light boat-rod with spinning guides and relic reel were just the right match for a hundred pounds or so of fish-beast that had swallowed a live bait intended for a king mackerel.

He had maneuvered his water bottle open to go with his lunch, a ham sandwich on white. Hardly the raw fish that Hemingway's hero subsisted on, and our fisherman would never dream of putting the line over his shoulder and risk a cut or worse. (Even in his most image-conscious phase, Hemingway probably would have left such things to his fictional fisherman.) The shark continued to pull the small boat over the nearly flat late-summer ocean. The tern that had dived at the bait just before the shark hit had gone elsewhere to hunt his food.

(In battling a shark of less than record proportions on old tackle, one really has nothing to lose. Nothing is at stake, but one does want to see the fish. Of course, in the case of a billfish or other top-water gamefish, it is most disappointing if the fish breaks off before one gets to see what it is. Such was the case once when we hooked a big ray or a cobia—we were not sure, even with that choice—that kept a friend of ours busy with 10-pound test spinning tackle for at least a half hour between the jetties. That one broke off before we were able to identify it for sure. Our shark didn't.)

Finally the shark was under the boat, and as is its wont, the fish circled many times before our angler could pump it into view. A fish coming out of the depths is always interesting, especially a big one. Like a silvery zeppelin it glided into view, its head at least a foot across.

What should be done with a big shark? It can be mounted as a trophy, landed and cut into small pieces for fish and chips, or tagged and released. Since the angler was alone, he had to compromise. He tightened the drag, the shark surged into the depths, and the line finally parted. It was time for a more leisurely draught from the water bottle. For some reason, the angler felt drained but elated, too.

Shark Notes: From the great white, blue, and mako sharks offshore, to the tiger, hammerhead, lemon, blacktip, and spinner sharks closer to the beach, anywhere along our coast where there is deep water in or close by the ocean, a variety of sharks may be caught. Surf fishermen fishing for trout or blues may see sharks in as little as three feet of water while the water is still warm in early fall. During the winter months, some coastal piers have resident populations of sharks that hang out near the fish-cleaning tables to feed on scraps. Most of the species of sharks that frequent the Atlantic coast are not maneaters, but no sensible person will swim at night or off the stern of a boat out in the Gulf Stream. Many piers and municipalities have rules banning sharkfishing, even though an experienced shark angler on a deserted beach or pier poses no real threat to anyone except himself and the shark. World records might be set on our Southeast coast, if shark fishermen could use the piers.

As soon as you are sure that the shark you have boated or beached is dead, cut diagonally down from behind its head to its anal spot and discard the head and guts, soaking the bottom half in seawater and icing it down promptly. Skin and fillet as soon as possible. Bleed larger sharks to get rid of the taste of urea. Clean and ice promptly. Before cooking, marinate the fillets in milk or a mixture of water, wine, and lemon juice. Cut the fillets into finger-size chunks and deep-fat fry. High protein, no bones, all meat. Delicious. Mako sharks are a delicacy, the old saying being that the fiercer the shark, the better it tastes on the table.

7

Spot: From the Piers to the Lagoons

A 1984 study by the National Marine Fisheries Service (NMFS) revealed that marine anglers fishing the inshore and offshore waters of the continental United States caught over 400 million fish in one year with an average weight of about a pound and a half. A lot of spot and other fish that rarely break a pound must have been included in the catch, which also proves that, as *Salt Water Sportsman* magazine put it, "the small game angler still predominates in the saltwater fishing world." The spot is a great example of a small game that everyone can play.

On an ordinary early fall afternoon on the piers of our Southeast coast, very few spot are caught that weigh more than half a pound. But when the fish move in word spreads fast. Anglers of all ages fish elbow to elbow. Whole families may line a small stretch of pier railing, sending one member of the tribe out for hot or cold drinks, depending on the weather, or for fresh bait, if the fish are hitting in great numbers. The word "tribe" is particularly fitting for spot fishermen since there are whole family groups of American Indians who make annual autumn spot fishing expeditions to the pier at Cherry Grove, returning to the coast their ancestors fished, enjoying themselves and catching a lot of fish. After all, someone has to pull the average down for all those 15-pound blues and 25-pound kings that go into the NMFS (say "nymphs") survey!

Spot fishing is by nature communal. Elbow room is all you will find on the pier during a run, but all you have to do is drop a line over the side—that old closed-faced Zebco spincast reel with eight-pound test line will do fine. An ounce of lead, two or three size 4 or 6 hooks baited with bloodworms, garden worms, or tiny pieces of shrimp, are all the bait and terminal tackle needed. It is usually not necessary to cast. Drop it in, feel a bite, and start reeling in fish, often two or three at a time. Coolers fill quickly, but make sure you have enough ice to keep the freshly caught spot fresh for the frying pan.

If there is no pier handy, most of the inlets along the coast and the Intracoastal Waterway close to saltwater provide good to excellent bankfishing. The lagoon behind South Carolina's Hunting Island State Park and a salt pond at Kiawah Island have provided my daughter and me some of our most memorable outings for spot. But any inlet along the Carolina and Georgia coast is a potential good fishing spot for spot when they make their fall runs. The spot is truly the fish for everyman—every woman and child, too!

For those who don't mind braving the water in late fall after

*Jennifer Johnsen and Donnie Millus found the brisk
weather of the day after Thanksgiving just right for some
spot fishing in a Carolina inlet. Clam baits on ultralight
tackle did the trick for the young lady from Virginia.*

the second cold snap, some of the best spot fishing of the year lies
in store. On one of those post-Thanksgiving trips, an old fishing
companion, Steve Johnsen of Virginia Beach, and I took his
daughter, Jennifer, and my younger son, Donnie, out to the mouth
of a Carolina inlet and anchored amidst "the fleet," an armada of
small boats that announced we were in the right place. Bundled
in their winter jackets, our youngsters fished with ultralight tackle
and freshly cut strips of clam and pulled in three or four fish for
every one taken by our neighbors. These were bigger spot, a few
of them going to three-quarters of a pound. With light line and
rods and the tide flowing in, each spot became the fighting
equivalent of a two-pound trout in freshwater. If you don't believe
me, try it yourself. Better still, try spot fishing with a youngster
who has no patience with patience. Spot fishing is its own instanta-
neous reward.

Do treat your spot with care, however, and don't catch more
than you can use. My favorite spot story is of a group of not too
sober anglers returning home from Myrtle Beach one evening.
They had stopped for fuel in Conway, some 15 miles from the

beach, when one of the locals noticed water dripping from the trunk of their old Chevy. The anglers were quick to open the trunk to exhibit their catch of which they were quite proud. There in the trunk, with no ice, were a few hundred pounds of spot. A preliminary sniff revealed that the fish had been there for the afternoon, baking in the hot trunk. "We've only got a two-hour ride home, so those fish should be fine," one of the tipsy fishermen noted with an optimistic grin. No doubt he did not receive a hero's welcome when he finished his journey.

8

The Fabulous Pompano, Ordinary Croaker, Mythical Sheepshead, and Jellyball-Eating Spadefish

The man was ecstatic. "I caught a cooler full of pompano," he announced as he came through the door of the tackle shop. Eyes were raised and, beers in hand, we crowded through the door and around his boat. It was a fancy bass rig with the high seats, not the best bet for fishing around a Carolina jetty, but when the fish are biting they don't care where you're sitting. Our proud friend, however, had been sitting and running his bass boat after a school of small jack crevalle, not pompano, the one member of the jack family that rates regular attention in *Gourmet* magazine. Pompano are delicious eating, even when they are not cooked in brown paper and served in a Louisiana setting.

Pompano are caught around coastal jetties and from our beaches, but they like warm water and they travel in schools that move around a lot. From a North Carolina or South Carolina pier or from the surf in the Carolinas and Georgia, they make excellent sport on light tackle, but special attention to fishing with very sharp hooks, fresh bait, and a careful attention to getting that live sand flea (mole crab) or small piece of shrimp into a slough in the beach on the rising tide or in that hole next to the jetty may produce the makings of a gourmet dinner. Pompano from a quarter of a pound to a few pounds in weight are not uncommon but certainly prized along the Southeast coast. Although anglers just taking potluck with shrimp or worm baits may take an occasional pompano, the angler who concentrates his fishing on this species with fresh sand fleas will be rewarded with fresh pompano—on occasion.

Croaker

Croaker and whiting will also hit both the sand flea and worm baits, both for surf and pier anglers. The croaker are probably more abundant. I have caught as many in mid-summer as in December. On some of the coldest days of the fall the croaker fishing can be outstanding from the piers along our coast, with fish of a pound or so not unusual. The giant croaker that anglers used to catch regularly in Chesapeake Bay are not as common on our Southeast coast, but a mess of half- to one-pounders taken from a coastal inlet or pier will make a dinner fit for a king. (By the way, if you're ever passing through my hometown, Conway, South Carolina, stop at the Ocean Fish Market behind the Jerry Cox Company and get yourself a "fish sandwich," flounder preferred but croaker a good option. For under two bucks [no tipping] you get two big croaker deep-fat fried and served with tartar sauce, salt and pepper [neither really needed], and three slices of bread. Be sure to lick the bones and your fingers clean. Yum!)

Sheepshead

My first headboat trip was out of Sheepshead Bay in Brooklyn, but the sheepshead runs of the last century which gave that harbor its name had become mere footnotes in local historians' works long before the fishing bug bit me. Down in Texas during my Army days at Fort Sam Houston I managed to catch one sheepshead during a weekend trip to Padre Island. Here in the Carolinas I continue to find the sheepshead the most elusive fish in the world. "You got to set the hook just before they bite," is the way one old-timer described pier fishing for sheepshead. The fish have big, strong teeth and little mouths designed to break clams or barnacles in a quick snapping bite. The angler whose tackle is not perfectly geared to sheepshead and whose reflexes are slow will rarely luck into one.

But there are people like the Reverend Robert Williams, a

retired preacher from Lexington, North Carolina, who makes a living fishing for sheepshead from our coastal piers. Well, not really a living, but a reminder to the rest of us that the right equipment and determination will do the trick. Williams fishes with a poolcue-stiff Daiwa graphite rod, a big reel loaded with fresh 40-pound test line, and his own terminal rigs consisting of wire leader, stainless steel hooks, and sliding egg-shaped sinkers to enable him to feel the bite and manhandle the fish. He lowers a sand flea ("You can keep them overnight but they don't keep too good after the sun comes out.") next to a pier piling "until you hit the bottom. Then you wind it up six to ten inches from the bottom. When he bites he will pick your bait up . . . set the hook then. If you don't, he will have your bait and be gone. If you hook him, get his head out of the water as soon as you can. Whatever you do, don't put your finger in his mouth. He has teeth like a sheep. That is where he got his name." Thus the gospel truth of sheepshead fishing, according to Reverend Williams. (Our

The sheepshead shows its "convict's stripes," befitting the fastest bait stealer on the Southeast coast. This one was taken next to the rocks at the mouth of South Carolina's Winyah Bay.

preacher even has heavy-duty shears to cut his mullet fillets for croaker bait, no doubt in the belief that God helps the fisherman who does his job well.)

At the jetties along our coast, particularly at Charleston, sheepshead anglers use long heavy calcutta poles, wire or heavy monofilament line, and fiddler crabs fished carefully right next to the rocks. Again it is a matter of having the right touch. After having my bait cleaned a dozen times in a row by sheepshead, I am tempted to mount a campaign to declare the sheepshead a mythical fish to go with the unicorn and the Grinch. They really do taste great, however, and my companions have had fun battling them, so if a knowledgeable angler offers to take you sheepshead fishing, accept the offer graciously but try to negotiate a commitment to split the catch in case your reflexes are not as quick as those of the sheepshead.

Spadefish

Spadefish look like angelfish from your aquarium that have been fed with a secret formula by a mad scientist until they are a thousand times bigger. When a seven-pound spadefish feels you set the hook and dives for the wreck over which it is feeding, your tackle had better be in good shape. After you fight this fish, assuming it hasn't taken your line around a buoy chain or the sharp edges of a sunken ship, the spadefish will leave you with an aching wrist. Like their deep-water distant cousin, the triggerfish, spadefish turn their bodies sideways, giving the angler an experience akin to fighting a mobile manhole cover.

It was thought by most fishermen on the Carolina and Georgia coast that spadefish, often seen calmly feeding along the top over an artificial reef, could not be caught on hook and line. Then one slow day on the Pawleys Island Reef, young Jimmy Orr, son of piscatorial prognosticator and general good guy J.B. Orr, noticed that the spadefish were feeding on jellyballs, those semi-firm jellyfish that feel like a soft rubber ball and keep their shape out of the water. He tried casting a small one to a spadefish, the fish hit it, and a new fishery had been discovered. Captain Buck Kempson passed the word to the South Carolina Marine Resources Department people and they have spread the recipe for taking spadefish on jellyballs, a combination that sounds funny but fights and tastes good—the fish, that is, not the bait.

Use heavy hooks (California Seabass is a good style) with a very

Teresa Stephens holds up her first spadefish of the day, caught on a jellyball bait.

small gap between point and shaft, for spadefish have small mouths. And wash your hands after handling the jellyballs because their secretions sting if you get them on sensitive parts of your body. My neck stung once because I had wiped my hands on a shirt that I later donned and the jellyball's poison was still there, not dangerous but annoying.

Next time you are fishing a reef or wreck and there are spadefish present, try a jellyball or a floated shrimp tail as bait. Casting a whole small jellyball on a baitcasting outfit (plop! splash!) to a cruising spadefish is not quite the equivalent of flycasting a Hairwinged Rat-Faced McDougal to a feeding Atlantic salmon, but take what nature gives you. Don't clean out the reef, however; leave a few of these odd-looking, delicate-feeding, hard-fighting, delicious-tasting spadefish for the next angler.

9

Deadly Devil Monster Rays

Every few years you can count on one of the popular outdoor magazines running an adventure story along with an artist's drawings of someone's tangle with a giant ray. "I held on tight to the handline as the monster ray towed my boat, me, and my frightened girl friend out to sea. But despite the threat of a severe thunderstorm and the knowledge that if the ray leaped and landed in our boat it could mortally injure us both, I was determined to hang on." And so on until with the help of a big winch the "deadly devil monster ray," now just a big dead manta ray, is hoisted on the dock, hung until it smells, and then towed out to sea for an unceremonious burial. Fortunately, most rays aren't that big. All of them deserve better treatment.

No one I have ever met will deliberately fish for rays, but a number of knowledgeable anglers will put one in the boat—very carefully—after an arm-tiring half hour or so, content in the knowledge that the ray is not only an impressive fish but the source of some excellent seafood. For years people have been eating scallops stamped out of the meaty flesh of filleted wing of ray and even if you know the source of the tasty white meat, you will still be licking your fingers after a dinner of fresh fried or baked ray fillets. Just watch out for the whiplike tail as you boat the fish and for the sharp stingers at the base of the spine of some rays. (If you are ever cut by a ray, despite your precautions, rinse the wound well in salt water, and have a medical person check it out as soon as possible. This same advice goes for bites from fish, nasty punctures from fins, and the unfortunate accidental hooking of an angler. All of these possibilities are rare, especially so for the people who use common sense when fishing.)

Summer and early fall bring many of these rays, ranging in weight from a few pounds to close to a hundred, around our bays, inlets, and piers. Blacktail and southern stingrays along with the cow-nosed (blunt rather than angular) ray are the most common, with the latter growing to sizes of 40 pounds or more. A 20-pounder will flap its wings forever, seemingly, as you try to hoist it out of the depths to see what you've hooked.

A smaller relative of the ray, the skate, has a long tail, somewhat like that of the shark, and a flat, triangular-shaped body. Skates are favorite baits of the shark fishermen, since they are commonly caught in the surf or from the piers. (The world record tiger shark, caught from one of our coastal piers, was taken on a skate rigged on a 16/0 hook.)

Usually the fisherman is drifting for flounder near an inlet mouth or anchored up and fishing cut or live mullet when a ray swims off with the bait. If the fisherman is not quick about pulling his anchor, all his line will go too. One quick surge, then a protracted struggle is the order of the day. If you are using less than 30-pound test line and you hook a fish in close to a pier or jetty and the fish just won't come to the surface, the odds are that it's a big cow-nosed ray.

One overcast July day as we drifted for flounder in the mouth of a Carolina inlet, we watched three men in a bass boat battle a ray on spinning tackle for at least half an hour. The ray kept its flat wide body and wings parallel to the bottom, and the combination of tide and water resistance made it slow work to pump the fish to the surface. Repeatedly the fish surged away from the man with the gaff. Finally the ray was gaffed, and one of the anglers showed his outdoor skills by shooting the ray with his pistol.

What happened next was not nice. "Hey you people want this fish?" one of them yelled over to a nearby boat. It was hard to believe, but they had killed a big old fish for no good reason. If they had enjoyed the fight, taken a picture, or just recorded their memories, and then released it to fight again, it would have been a plus for mankind and nature both. But, no, they had to kill the old scavenger not for food but just because it had gotten in their way. If there was nobody handy to take the carcass it would be dumped back into the sea. Sad. No one in any of the nearby boats seemed eager to clean someone else's shot fish.

Even though the ray provides excellent eating, a lot of knowledgeable fishermen prefer to just battle the fish to the boat and cut the line, secure in the knowledge that the ray will live to fight another day and perhaps put chills into onlookers as it cruises under a boat or alongside a pier, often in the company of two or three of its fellows. That massive blip on your liquid crystal recorder may not be a school of fish but one big ray that could translate into 25 pounds of scalloplike fillets or an hour of wrist-wringing fish fighting on what would otherwise be a slow day. If you do decide to boat the ray, please remember two things: be careful of the tail and make sure you plan to cut out the good meat. It's a shame to waste, even if the fish really isn't the "deadly devil monster ray" of the magazines.

10

My Last Grouper

The image of southeastern offshore bottom fishing for many anglers from the North is often one of anglers taking giant red snapper and grouper from an offshore reef. Yet offshore reefs are few and far between, and snapper and grouper are becoming more and more scarce on these reefs as commercial and sportfishing pressure limits itself to that small part of the offshore bottom that does support magnificent creatures like the grouper. At five or six or more dollars per pound, not even Dean Swift's Irish children would avoid extinction for long. Such is the sad story of our various groupers, a race of giants that have grown smaller over the years and increasingly rare.

Take the case of my last glorious grouper, fittingly caught on the first deep-sea trip possible after Hurricane Gloria had rudely flaunted her skirts in our face. It was a bright, brisk Saturday—too brisk in my opinion—for the northeast winds that had been guaranteed to die down just never did stop swelling our seas and rocking the boat. Perched in the bow of the headboat was a contingent of anglers from Western Ontario University, visiting with us for U.S.C.-Coastal Carolina College's twelfth annual inter-collegiate fishing match and seminar. Joining them were Mitch Godwin and son Sean and my younger son, Donnie, and I. Captain Don Lash of the "Summer Sun" out of Murrells Inlet put us and 40 other passengers over a good piece of bottom in 110 feet of water and tooted the horn to signal "lines down."

The scene was being repeated that day all along the North Carolina, South Carolina, and Georgia coasts by dozens of headboats and private boats. Following Loran numbers, captains would be hoping that their favorite reef would produce steady fishing for four or five hours, with perhaps a genuine red snapper or a nice grouper for show and tell back at the dock. Twenty years ago the grouper would have been a certainty, ten years ago a good bet, but today it is only a hope. The fishable offshore reefs are divided among an increasing number of recreational and commercial fishermen.

I had brought a "live line" rod to fish for kings if the bottom fishing was slow. To pass the time until someone took a tomtate, a small fish I could use for live bait, I took one of the boat rods and dropped down two seabass hooks baited with pieces of squid hardly the size of quarters. There was a tap. I struck at what would probably be a silver snapper and was rewarded by having the rod bend and point down to the water. The drag gave a noise between screech and whirr and I mentally complimented Captain Lash on his good taste in fishing holes. On 40-pound test line the grouper was surging away repeatedly and alternating this tactic with what seemed like runs toward the surface. (Grouper, by the way, are occasionally caught on lures run behind deep planers fished over deep reefs and drops by king mackerel anglers. In other words, this is an aggressive feeder, not limiting itself to the bottom, another reason that commercial or "sport" fishermen can clean a reef out of big grouper if they anchor over it for a day or night of serious fishing.)

By the time the fish lay gasping on the surface I had yelled five times for the gaff. The fish bobbing on the surface reminded me of the big codfish we used to catch off the Rhode Island coast or the huge catfish of the Santee-Cooper lakes, all the fight gone as the behemoth awaits the gaff or the net. Fortunately for our slow starting mate, the fish was firmly hooked in the side of its mouth. I was a little disappointed when he announced to me that I had caught the pool fish. I have nothing against winning a friendly side bet to help swell the crews' tips, but it gave me little to look forward to for the rest of the day if this was the biggest grouper he had seen all season, as he claimed.

(Dr. Gene Huntsman of the National Marine Fisheries Service in Beaufort, North Carolina, has been studying the grouper and snapper in our offshore waters for years, and he is somewhat less pessimistic, although he admits that the grouper or snapper fishing is not what it was 20 or 30 years ago. Captain Steven Speros of the "Hurricane" out of North Myrtle Beach reported good grouper fishing this past fall, "after the weather finally cooled off," and the "Carolina Princess" out of Morehead City had the same experience.)

Charley Abshire of Little River, South Carolina, with the only two grouper of a slow day's fishing on the "Boss Hogg." Silver snapper (red porgy) made up the bulk of the day's catch.

My fish weighed 17 pounds, the largest grouper I have caught in my dozen years of fishing this coast. Others have caught larger fish and will continue to do so, but each year the odds against any given angler on a headboat catching a bigger one grow slimmer. If you do go out on a Carolina headboat, don't let the success of your trip depend on catching a grouper. But if you do, enjoy the fight and the prospect of grouper steaks cooked to perfection. The lordly grouper deserves at least that. Like tall trees and wide beaches, grouper are more likely to be ravaged by man than by nature. That there will be big grouper offshore for our grandchildren to catch is greatly to be wished, for the grouper is a bruising battler that every angler of the seas should encounter at least once.

Light tackle and small pieces of shrimp, worms, or cut bait do the trick for whiting (sea mullet), a small but delicious bottomfeeder caught from the piers and the surf all along the Southeast coast.

11

Sea Mullet, Whiting, and Baseball

The whiting that Northern fishermen know is a totally different species of fish from the kingfish or king whiting that pier and surf fishermen love to catch along the Carolina and Georgia coasts. The northern whiting or silver hake is actually a member of the cod family, and with its taper from fat head to skinny tail it has won the sobriquet of "baseball bat." Our whiting, known along the upper reaches of the Southeast coast as "sea mullet" or "Virginia mullet," does have one quality that has always reminded me of baseball bats: despite their small size they smack the bait solidly.

Whiting, which average only a half-pound or so—a two-pounder is an outstanding fish—may be caught from the surf, piers, and from small boats just offshore. They prefer a moving bait—small pieces of mullet, shrimp, bloodworms, or even garden worms will do—and will usually hit the bait hard and hook themselves. On light tackle one gets the feeling that something weighing a few pounds has hit the bait, rather than a 12-inch whiting.

Once one gets into a school of whiting, it's hard to quit, for they are not only fun to hook and play, but they are one of the most delicious of bottom fish. R.D. Brigham, the genial proprietor of City Bait and Tackle in Myrtle Beach, attributes their flavor to the slight touch of iodine, natural rather than added, that the fish has. My experience is that youngsters who don't normally enjoy fish will clean a plate of tenderly fried or broiled whiting fillets without having to be urged.

Spring through fall provides good to excellent fishing for whiting. On a day when the kings are far out at sea and the flounder and spottail aren't feeding eagerly, a fishing trip may be saved with half a cooler full of freshly caught whiting. Although the fillets may be frozen, whiting caught, iced down, cleaned, and cooked the same day are a treat that even the most demanding gourmand would find hard to resist.

Whiting Notes: Freshly cut bait, two-hook bottom rigs with freshly sharpened size 4 or 6 Eagle Claw hooks, and bouncing the bait as you drift just offshore—whiting like sandy bottoms—should get results. From the pier, cast toward the surf, bounce the bait with a slow retrieve, pausing for five seconds before raising the rod tip. In the surf, whiting will hit small sand fleas or mole crabs: Peel off a little bit of the shell and fish the bait on a tight line just over the first drop.

12

Amberjack, Toughest Fish on the Wreck

As we slowly trolled past the buoy marking the eastern edge of the artificial reef, a crowd began to gather behind our live baits. The crowd was unruly, pushy, even savage, for it was a school of amberjack, "Georgetown Tuna" to anglers who have discovered that these bruisers love the rough neighborhood of the many wrecks off Georgetown, South Carolina. But the scene could have been repeated all along the North Carolina and South Carolina coasts and off the Georgia Sea Islands. The waters erupted as six amberjack, their collective weight some three or four hundred pounds, fought over four live bluefish and mullet trailing from our small boat. Splash, splash, smash, chug, screech, "grab that rod, no, that one, keep the boat moving," snap, snap. Damage report: two lines broken, two fish on, both under the boat and diving in different directions. Tom Owens, vacationing from Illinois, was into a sea monster that was anything but relaxing. I was into its twin and our lines were crossed. The only other person in the boat, Tom's daughter, Nancy, was already maneuvering the boat away from the reef, inducing the amberjack into open water where the anglers had at least a fighting chance of landing one.

The amberjack may well be the easiest big game fish to hook but one of the toughest to put in the boat, particularly if you hook him over an artificial reef constructed with barges that he knows as home. "First thing he does," notes charter skipper Ray Scribner, "is dive for the wreck. The next thing he does is break your line. I find amberjack a low percentage fish. My customers love 'em."

Over artificial reefs and wrecks, on offshore reefs, and even off the piers, 40- to 80-pound amberjack are not rare in the Carolinas. Headboat customers regularly are jolted to the rail as they set the hook on a big amberjack while expecting only the resistance of a 5-pound vermilion snapper or a 15-pound scamp grouper. "Pool goes to the amberjack," intoned the mate of the "Captain Stacy IV," a Morehead City headboat decorated with stringers of brightly colored vee-liners interspersed with grouper and silver snapper. No doubt the angler collected his money but left the fish for the crabs. Unfortunately, most of the larger amberjack along our coasts are infected with wormlike parasites. On the other hand, perhaps it is fortunate for amberjack and for coastal anglers, for it makes it a lot easier to release that monster when the prospect of food for the table is small. (For those amberjack that are hooked too deeply to survive, anglers may take a strip of delicious, parasite-free flesh from along both sides of the back by cutting down from the fins and wedging the knife in from the side. The rest of the amberjack may be filleted for outstanding grouper bait or ground for chum.)

But back to our two bruisers. We had been looking for the last kings of the inshore fishing season on a Veterans' Day afternoon that gave us bright sunshine and a sea dappled by only the softest of Indian summer breezes. But just as the amberjack saves an occasional charter boat skipper's day by providing enough excitement to carry most customers through the cold of winter, so this pair of "greater" (their technical first name) amberjack was determined to test our skills and stamina. Their Latin name, *Seriola dumerili*, even sounds tough! And they were both taking line off our reels at will.

As Nancy eased the boat away from the buoy and the safety—for the amberjack—of the reef, I started wrapping my rod around Tom's to get the lines uncrossed. That done, I tightened up as hard as I could on the drag of my ocean-sized Ambassadeur and began pumping the rod, gaining five or six feet of line by raising the rod and reeling fast as I lowered it. In about 10 minutes I saw the fish again, not the foam-surrounded fighter that was diving for my bait across the surface, but a torpedo-shaped streak of yellow and copper coming grudgingly out of the depths. The vanity of an angler's trust in his skills and efforts was made obvious in the next instant as the amberjack simply decided to dive to the bottom and stay there. "I prefer not to" be moved, be taken, come near the boat—whatever. This is the Bartleby of fishes, and your aching wrist is of no concern to him.

Even on 17-pound test line, a 60-pound amberjack away from his line-destroying wreck will eventually be brought to the boat. Nancy slips the gaff in the fish's lower jaw and as I attempt to cut the wire I get lucky: The single hook and two trailing trebles flip loose. I let the fish rest, no, I rest for a minute, and swing it into the boat, gently, for I want this fish to live, placing the amberjack across the deck at the stern. The amberjack fills the boat with his immense power, but does not flip around. The fight has exhausted him, too. A yellow tag, #04456—provided in this case by the South Carolina Wildlife Department, Marine Resources Division; other tag sources are listed in the appendix—is inserted behind his dorsal fin and I swing the fish back into the water, holding him in the flow of the ocean as we both, the creature of the land and the creature of the ocean, replenish our oxygen supply. I turn the gaff hook down, freeing the fish, and the amberjack dives for the bottom, sporting a yellow plastic i.d. tag that may bring us word a year or two from now that the fish did live to fight another day.

Meanwhile, Tom has wisely let his fish run, and he now pumps the other exhausted giant slowly toward the boat. It is even bigger than mine, I say 60 pounds, the Owenses 70. (Who's bigger, the football Giants' left or right tackle? The quarterback about to be sacked doesn't ask, nor should we.) We will never weigh this one. I reach over with the pliers to cut the wire leader and release the fish, making a mental note to bring more tags tomorrow. The kings may be gone for the year, but a battle with a greater amberjack will bring us back to the reef tomorrow.

13

Billfish, Wahoo, Dolphin, and Tuna

We were 60 miles out in the Atlantic, five minutes after nine on the Saturday of a Labor Day weekend, five minutes into a three-day billfish tournament, one of dozens held annually on the Southeast coast. A half-second ago a white marlin had given one last flip of his powerful tail to drive him out of the water, his mouth open, to engulf a dead mullet rigged to look like a live mullet as it was trolled behind our boat. In the next second or two the following occurred: the waters erupted, the bait disappeared, the mate yelled "fish on," and the pulse rates of everyone on our boat accelerated. I happened to be relaxing in the fighting chair, but the next thing I knew I was holding a rod attached by a few hundred yards of monofilament line to a leaping marlin.

The next 15 minutes were exciting, exhausting, demanding, and punishing while we were worrying, coaxing, cooperating, hoping, praying, cursing (but just mildly), encouraging, complaining, criticizing, and eventually congratulating each other when the fish was gaffed and put in the boat.

The next three days were boring, frustrating, mutually recriminating, tiring then exhausting, painstaking, experimenting, filled with hope, and finally disappointing. On the third day (getting up at three in the morning gets old quickly during a tournament), just before the final "lines up," the devil threw in another white marlin that charged away with the teaser as four gentlemen and a gentle lady screamed at the mate to set the hook on the fish leaping with the lure in its mouth. The mate was calmly pointing out that none of the rods were bent and that it was impossible to set the hook on a fish that was not attached to the boat. We were not in the mood to listen to his rational discourse, however.

Such are the joys and miseries of offshore big-game fishing, "hours of boredom followed by minutes of panic"—just one version of the old offshore sportfishing saw. As I looked down from the tuna tower of a Florida-based sportfishing boat one spring afternoon, the water behind our boat (we were some 70 miles off Charleston, South Carolina) parted for what looked like an oversized torpedo. It was a blue marlin, longer than the average Volkswagen, but quite noncommittal with regard to our baits. The previous day the crew I was with—this was in the old Gulf Stream Marina-Pabst Billfish Tournament—had two strikes and boated one fish. Two days before there was nothing but big bull dolphin to hit our lures. Billfishing is a chancey proposition.

Billfishing is also an expensive proposition, with more and more fishing days required to get the same number of strikes. There are, to put it simply, not as many blue and white marlin and swordfish as there used to be. Commercial longliners have taken them by the hundreds of thousands, sportfishermen have taken

A blue marlin is weighed in at a billfish tournament in the 1970s. More and more tournaments are going to "tag and release" competition to protect the decreasing stock of billfish available to sport fishermen.

them by the thousands, and billfish populations have declined drastically. It's as simple as that. Tough enough that a hundred thousand dollars is not an unusual investment in a good offshore sportfishing boat with electronics and tackle to match, but the billfish population has also dwindled from those days barely two decades ago when the waters off the Carolinas and Georgia were, if not virgin, certainly quite fruitful. Fads such as nighttime fishing with chemical glow sticks to attract swordfish to baits drifted deep or live-bait slow trolling for marlin during the day will mean a few more fish for experimenting anglers, but the overall trend still continues downward. If you don't believe me, ask any fisherman who has run his own boat for billfish off the Southeast coast for at least 10 years.

The late Oscar Vick set a South Carolina record with this wahoo, proudly held up by his son Stan, now an officer with the South Carolina Wildlife and Marine Resources Department.

Some solace for the decline in billfishing is provided by the tuna, big yellowfins that fight well and taste good, but drive tournament billfishermen to distraction by crashing carefully rigged baits meant for the billfish. Another fish that means fun and fine dining is the wahoo, the bigger, better-tasting (arguably) cousin of the king mackerel. My impression of the wahoo is that a huge, angry jaw has emerged from the depths ready to devour the swimming bait but eager to make it die of fright even before the savage strike. Wahoo, of course, are not named after a fisherman's excited yell, but, more likely, after the Pacific island of Oahu where they first came to the attention of Western man.

In the later part of the last decades of the twentieth century, tuna, wahoo, and dolphin will continue to be much more likely rewards for an offshore fishing trip than billfish, and one does not have to justify bringing such fish back to the dock for "show and tell" by mounting them, since they make for excellent eating. Mounting a billfish has drawbacks: not only is it an expensive testimony to man's vanity, but as an experienced angler noted, pointing to the blue marlin on his office wall, most wives will tolerate your mounting only one billfish. After that, tag and release makes good sense, and the trend in billfish tournaments is entirely toward tagging and releasing such fish. But even the food value of such offshore beauties as the dolphin, which has most of the colors of the rainbow in life but turns a dull yellow in death, should not turn an angler into a fill-the-box-frenzy that won't stop as long as there is one more peanut dolphin left in a school behind the boat. Excuses such as "I want to take care of so and so who had a poor trip with me recently" are weak: let so-and-so come out and catch a few himself.

A charter trip for billfish may cost close to a thousand dollars, but it is still an adventure, even though the days of the pioneers on our last frontier, the waters offshore, are over. A camera to take a picture of a freshly tagged marlin about to be released will save you the expense of having a fish mounted or the spiritual pain of sneaking one off to the garbage dump at night. Sadly, the latter (or "donating" the carcass to the local prison farm or state penitentiary) has been too often the case and we are all the poorer for it.

Sailfish Note: The sailfish is perhaps the most beautiful of the billfish and is often, at least from North Carolina's Cape Lookout to Georgia's offshore waters, the billfish most likely to show up unexpectedly and surprise an angler just 10 miles off the beach. In recent years, late August off Cape Fear, North Carolina, provided some surprises for king mackerel fishermen in the form of sailfish leaping on slow-trolled live menhaden.

14

Striped Bass: The Southeast Coast Sanctuary

My guest was a fisherman from the Eastern Shore of Virginia who had taken stripers at Cape Cod, Montauk Point, Sandy Hook, and Chesapeake Bay. As his graphite rod twitched with our first strike of the day, George Reiger leaned into his first coastal Carolina striper, rockfish to many coastal residents, a feisty four-pounder that he patiently brought to the boat, a freshwater fish that looked as clean, shining, and fat as any netted by the first Indians who fished our rivers before white settlers came to these shores.

The night before, Reiger had been the featured speaker at the South Carolina Wildlife Federation Banquet in Myrtle Beach. He had planned to fly out early in the morning, but changed his plans abruptly when I told him that I thought the next morning would be ideal for winter striper fishing. The chance for good striped bass fishing didn't come often anymore to fishermen on the northern part of the Atlantic coast. Later, as he netted a 13-pounder for me, he noted that some Northerners would be envious if they knew such good striped bass fishing still existed. Overhead, crossing the Intracoastal Waterway by bridge, vacationers were heading south on U.S. Highway 17. Legally, we were fishing saltwater; in fact, it was brackish and close to fresh at low tide, the ideal habitat for Southeast coast striped bass.

Even though the last century has seen a cyclical movement of striped bass populations north of Cape Hatteras, the early 1980s brought bad news to striped bass fishermen along the Atlantic coast. Stocks had dwindled due to overfishing and pollution, charter boat fishing had collapsed, prospects were bleak and getting worse. Striped bass, perhaps too late, were recognized as a gamefish very much in danger. Drastic limits were imposed, even to the extent of banning all fishing for striped bass in some areas.

As Reiger pointed out, the fishermen of our Southeast coast are fortunate that the striped bass here is alive and well. When I finish writing this chapter I may hitch up my boat, drive 20 miles to the Intracoastal Waterway near the North Carolina-South Carolina border, and fish for stripers on light spinning tackle for a few hours until it gets dark. Since the water is clean and the December weather clear and mild, I would not be surprised if I came home with two or three fat, clean, native, unstocked striped bass that had no chemical residues in them and would make not only for a good fight but great tablefare. Average size would be about 3 pounds, but I have seen more fish over 12 pounds taken from the Intracoastal Waterway and our coastal rivers in the past few years than I had seen in the previous decade at the fabled Santee-Cooper lakes.

The striped bass in our area along the Southeast coast is not a saltwater fish. Most fishermen know about the once phenomenal and still reliable (thanks to good management) striper fishing at South Carolina's Santee-Cooper lakes. When Lakes Marion and Moultrie were formed by the damming of the Santee River, stripers were trapped by the dam, but in an ideal environment for fish that had adapted to living in freshwater hundreds if not thousands of years before. Because of the flow of the rivers coming into the upper lake (Marion), Santee-Cooper striped bass were able to reproduce (striper eggs need flowing water to float in after they are fertilized) and the presence of excellent forage in the form of herring made the Santee-Cooper lakes a nursery for great striper populations. But it was no miracle. The Southeast coast striped bass that adapted to life in these lakes had long before opted for life in freshwater, moving down toward the ocean in the winter and back up the rivers in the summer. Although occasionally one may catch our coastal striped bass in saltwater, they are rarely caught anyplace else but in our coastal rivers, at least south of Cape Hatteras. (I have yet to hear of anyone who can testify to a striped bass being taken in the surf or from the ocean piers of the South Carolina and Georgia coasts, and I would like to hear from anyone who has taken a striper from the beaches or ocean piers

The author with a mid-winter striper taken on a white "Mister Twister" grub from the Intracoastal Waterway near the North Carolina–South Carolina border. The skimobile suit has made fishing the Southeast coast a comfortable proposition even during the winter months, given half a break with the weather.

Photo by George Reiger

of North Carolina south of Beaufort Inlet.) What we have is a race of stripers that will venture down toward saltwater but not "past the breakers," as my Carolina neighbors would put it.

Stripers may be taken in the Intracoastal Waterway and coastal rivers in the Carolinas and Georgia year-round, but late fall through early March is the best time. Trolled white "Swimmin' Grubs," green "Mister Twister" grubs with their vibrating tails, and combinations of "Rebel" plugs and grubs or "Smilen Bill" bucktails all work wonders on the right tide. Fishing the pilings around bridges can also be excellent. Since few people fish for stripers, it may pay to experiment, but these healthy freshwater stripers of our Southeast coastal rivers will often reward the angler with excellent sport and tablefare.

The cloud on the horizon for anglers who enjoy coastal river striper fishing is population growth. For example, water and sewer authorities in just two counties in coastal South Carolina, Horry and Georgetown, are authorized to discharge 20 million gallons of treated effluent into the Intracoastal Waterway every day, according to the Myrtle Beach *Sun News.* Even if this effluent is treated, the chemicals used to clean it are not conducive to the survival of striped bass and other fish. Such discharges will grow and become more common, unfortunately. Only if North Carolina, South Carolina, and Georgia can carefully protect and manage the striped bass they still have in their coastal rivers can the Southeast coast remain a sanctuary for both the striped bass and striper fishermen, two endangered species.

15

Everybody's Favorite Family: The Drums

Bass and trout fishermen are in the majority among the American angling public, but I feel sorry for them if they have never tangled with the bass and trout of the Carolina and Georgia coasts. Our bass have spots on their tails and pound for pound are probably three times tougher fighters (maybe four if the water temperature is right) than largemouth or smallmouth bass. Besides, how many freshwater bass fishermen get to net 20- or 30-pounders every year or so? Our trout are just as pretty, their black spots standing out against pink, silver, and touches of blue and green, and a six-pounder running across an incoming tide is a testimony to the inherent power of the wild fish of saltwater.

Of course, both our "bass," also known as spottails, channel bass, or red drum, and our "trout," also d.b.a. spotted sea trout or winter trout, are distant cousins in the drum family and one of the mainstays of sportfishing along our Carolina and Georgia coasts. Throw in the gray trout or weakfish, alias "summer trout," and the bruising black drum that may tow your boat around one of our sounds or rivers, and you have quite a family, although other related members will be welcome in most anglers' coolers.

Think of the black drum as the heavyweight of the family, cruising the bottom of deep sounds and demanding that your 4/0

reel and rod to match be in good shape and y...
But smaller members of the family—any bla...
pounds should be released unless you wish to...
for its food value is not high—will frequently...
fishing with pieces of shrimp or cut bait such...
bottom along our Carolina jetties.

The red drum is more abundant and easier to... ...
the 90 pounder taken at Hatteras Island Pier some years ago is
not likely to be matched south of Cape Lookout, 30 pounders are
caught every year from the beaches and inlets of the Carolina and
Georgia coasts. The red drum can be taken 12 months a year,
given a mild winter, for it will stay in the inlets all winter if there
is no sustained deep freeze. Although larger fish are taken on
whole spot or big chunks of fresh mullet, metal lures, plugs, and
plastic grubs will take a lot of these fish.

I originally used two-inch grubs with spade-shaped tails, and
occasionally have caught fish on sickled twister tails. Grub tails
are oval shaped and hang down almost perpendicular to the axis
of the lure. Since the foot, or tail, of the lure presents nearly a
half-inch square area of resistance to the water, even the slightest
movement of the lure causes it to vibrate. If the puppy drum are
around the rocks in summer or fall, grubs are often the best bet.

My favorite red drum—on my stretch of the South Carolina
coast they are "spottail bass" but this one really qualified as a
"channel bass,"—was the first fish ever caught in the New World
by a British angler who was visiting here a few years ago. Dr.
Richard Koesterer of U.S.C.-Coastal Carolina College invited me
over one summer evening for a party in honor of a former
colleague, Dr. Alan Drew of the University of London. I offered
to take them with me on a king mackerel expedition the next
morning, provided that they could get up at 5 A.M. after a night
of moderately riotous living. As I cast a net for bait just after
dawn, my companions sipped at the black coffee their host had
thoughtfully provided and complained about the early hour. I
complained because I couldn't catch any big mullet to troll for
kings, but perhaps that was in the hands of Providence. At the
north jetty of Murrells Inlet the tide was just right, not for kings,
but for spottail, and I decided to give our little finger mullet a
try. On a spaghetti-thin graphite rod from Shakespeare, a small
"Thumbar" Ambassadeur reel, and 20-pound test "Stren" line,

hooked into what turned out to be a 35-pound channel bass, e outstanding catch in that year's Grand Strand Fishing Rodeo. What is more amazing is that we had the fish in the boat in 10 minutes, when most experts insist, and rightly so, that it generally takes one minute per pound to beach a spottail. I "cheated," however; when Drew reeled the fish toward the boat the first time, it dived under the boat. The next time I held the landing net way down in the water and the fish dived right into it.

Although such hefty red drum are fun, a school of three-pound fish that are in the mood to hit a smoke-colored grub just gently pulled off the rocks by an angler casting from an anchored or slowly moving boat will make for more lasting excitement and better eating. Float fishing with live shrimp, casting the barrier islands and beaches with cut mullet, or fishing live finger mullet on sliding sinker rigs also does the trick.

When I was first getting into saltwater fishing as a teenager on Long Island, weakfish were quite rare. By the time I had returned from Vietnam, weakfish of five pounds were common occurrences off the beaches of Connecticut where I did most of my fishing when graduate school wasn't in session. When I moved to the Carolinas in the early 1970s I soon learned that weakfish were "summer trout" and that the best fishing for them was in the middle of winter, given mild weather and a lighted pier. I have since taken them in every month of the year, with December the best month for large numbers, although the fish average not much more than a pound, at least off our coastal piers.

Bigger ones do show up, however. One May day a student of mine delivered the fishing professor's equivalent of an apple for the teacher: he reported to me that he had taken three summer trout averaging over nine pounds from one of our coastal jetties. The next day the fish were gone. I told him that the previous November we had taken some five pounders in the same area, but the spring visit was apparently short although sweet. At that same spot the following spring I was trolling for a small bluefish to be used as live bait for kings when I hooked a fish that ran all over the place and would not come to the net. I thought it was a big spottail until I got it into the net and noticed that it had no spots to speak of: it was a weakfish of close to 10 pounds, the largest I have taken down here.

Summer trout may be taken on cut bait or lures, with green

grubs or jigged Hopkins spoons particularly effective in the late fall. The fish make for good eating, although their cousins the "winter trout" or spotted sea trout are preferred by most fishing gourmets on our coast.

It is not by chance that I have saved the winter trout for last. It is my favorite fish, no matter how powerful the billfish, no matter how majestic the king, no matter how solid the flounder, nor how tough the spottail. Winter trout are simply beautiful to behold and challenging to catch. Cast a strip of fresh mullet in the surf along the Carolina or Georgia coast in early fall and you may take a few, more if you get into a school of them feeding up the beach on an incoming tide. But go stalking the winter trout at one of our inlets—New or Topsail or Masonboro, or Carolina Beach, or Little River, or Murrells, or North or Trenchards—or from any island—Bald Head or Pawleys or Capers or Parris or Fripp or Hilton Head or Tybee or Wassaw or Sapelo or any

Johnny McDowell holds up a stringer of November spotted sea trout, caught on "Mirrolure" plugs while trolling in a coastal inlet. Good trout fishing runs in cycles. This catch was made in 1979. Saltwater trout fishing declined in the next few years, only to improve dramatically in 1985.

other—wading and casting, trolling a lure or casting one from a boat, or anchoring a boat and fishing with live shrimp. Feel that strike which may be just the tiniest of taps and yet come from a seven-pound spotted sea trout that has just swallowed your lure or bait completely. Hold your rod high as the fish throbs against it, surging away so fast that if your drag is too light or your line just a bit old—the latter, by his own admission, cost Lem Winesett three big fish in a row one frosty autumn morning—you have lost the fish.

But hang on and the trout surges away, your reel sings a smooth song amid the clean, cool air of a late autumn afternoon, and slowly, grudgingly, there comes to the surface a majestic fish, its dorsal fin erect, its spotted sides ranging from white and silver underneath to green and blue above. Five pounds of winter trout takes line two or three more times before you slide it into the net. No better honor to a fish than to stuff it and bake it for a holiday feast. The winter trout, most royal member of the drum family, deserves no less, often the last best fish before Christmas and the first memorable one of a springlike February day on our Southeast coast.

16

Big Game Fishing's Greatest Catch

The following true story of Walter Maxwell's world-record tiger shark is reprinted with permission of Times Mirror Magazines, Inc., from the April, 1984, issue of Outdoor Life *magazine. Copyright 1984 Times Mirror Magazines, Inc. This story was voted first prize in the annual contest for members of the Outdoor Writers Association of America, sponsored by the Shakespeare Fishing Tackle Company of Columbia, South Carolina.*

The tiger shark was 10 times heavier than the muscular stone-mason who was bracing his 190-pound, six-foot body against the shark's first run. His 16/0 big-game reel gave line grudgingly and his heavy rod bent in a tight arc as the shark surged away from the pier with a huge hook embedded in its jaw. A multistrand, wire leader and 130-pound-test line connected the shark with the man who was soon to set a world record that still stands—and do it from a fishing pier, not a well-equipped boat.

It was the afternoon of Saturday, June 13, 1964, and the beach near Cherry Grove pier, north of Myrtle Beach, South Carolina, was dotted with vacationers enjoying the sand and surf. Most of them paid no attention to the angler far out on the pier. The tiger shark had taken the bait at about 2 P.M. and the rapid-fire *click* of the reel had galvanized Walter Maxwell and his shark fishing friends. Maxwell put the butt of his rod into the socket of his rod belt and clipped the custom-made shoulder harness to the rings of his reel. He and the shark were locked in combat. Maxwell had great respect for big sharks. He had seen sharks that were brought to the pier grab pilings in their jaws.

The first run of Maxwell's first giant shark was, in his words, ". . . strong, steady, unconcerned. I let him run several hundred yards." Surprisingly, Maxwell was able to fight the shark back to the pier several times. After an hour of runs by the shark and Maxwell's muscular pumping and reeling, the shark was alongside the pier.

Maxwell still thinks that his first tiger shark came in too easily. "I believe," he told me, "that a really big shark doesn't feel threatened very much by feeling the hook and that the shark will swim toward the fisherman to see what's holding him."

Whatever the reason, Maxwell's strength and the shark's apparent unconcern put one of Maxwell's friends in danger. Jim Michie, from Columbia, South Carolina, had fished for sharks on Padre Island in Texas and had helped introduce Walter Maxwell to shark fishing from piers. Michie stood ready with a 16-foot, fiberglass vaulter's pole solidly attached to a huge gaff hook. But the pole and stainless-steel gaff hook were not enough to hold that huge shark after a fight that had lasted only an hour. The shark was "green"—fresh and untired.

"None of us realized how big that fish really was," Michie recalled. "When I leaned over the railing to set the gaff, I thought 'My God, I'll never be able to hold this fish.' The thing looked like a cow wallowing in the heavy swells. It was about 18 feet in length and must have gone at least 2,500 pounds."

Michie was pulled tight against the railing of the pier when the gaffed tiger thrashed in the swells. Then Maxwell's hooks pulled free and Michie was left trying to hold the shark with only the gaff. No human being could hold such a monster with its strength still unspent. With the fall of a wave, the gaff was pulled from Michie's hands and Maxwell's first tiger shark was free. It swam

A hand-crafted leather harness, Penn Senator reel, and Shakespeare rod, plus a 14/0 hook, and a skate (a ray-like fish) for bait, were essential equipment for the assault on the world record. (That's a larger 20/0 hook Maxwell is holding in this 1983 photo. He believes that there are still plenty of sharks around that are big enough to swallow such a hook, if only pierfishing for monster sharks were still allowed.)

out to sea with the gaff still embedded in its mouth and the pole jutting above the waves.

Even though Maxwell wanted to set a world record, he was out for sport, too. "I was fishing for sport, and losing one fish didn't interfere with that," he said.

Maxwell and his friends dreamed of catching a world-record shark from a pier. The fact that big sharks could be taken from shore was well known to a few anglers, such as Jim Michie, who had done it himself. It was easier to fish for sharks from the pier than from the beach. You could fish the whole weekend—day and night—from a pier more easily than you could fish from a boat, and for a lot less money.

"As far as we were concerned, the pier was our only possible chance at a big shark," Maxwell recalled.

Maxwell, Michie, and another South Carolinian, M.C. Meetze, spent many summer weekends on the Cherry Grove pier. They often slept there, but they were always alert for the alarmlike click of their big-game reels. They had studied the International Game Fish Association (IGFA) rules for establishing an all-tackle record. Among many other stipulations, the rules specified that no one was allowed to touch the angler or his equipment while he was battling the fish. In other words, no one could help the angler to fight the fish.

Maxwell is quick to give his friends credit, though. "Michie knew a lot about fishing for sharks," Maxwell recalled recently. "He had 9/0 and 12/0 reels that were big enough to use for monster sharks, but I decided to invest in my own rod and reel. Michie built the rod for me using a 39-thread, Shakespeare, fiberglass blank with Mildrum guides. It was designed for shark fishing."

Meetze's big contribution was a hand-crafted fighting harness made out of half a cowhide with one-inch-wide leather straps that would not cut into the angler's shoulders. Maxwell's final piece of equipment was a wide, leather rod belt with a socket for the rod butt.

Maxwell's 16/0 Penn Senator reel was about the size of a bowling ball, and was filled with 1,400 yards of Ashaway Dacron line, testing 130 pounds. The line was strong enough to anchor a fair-size boat.

After the loss of Maxwell's first tiger shark on Saturday, no more big sharks were hooked that day. Evening came, and then night, and the curious onlookers that had gathered to watch the battle between man and shark drifted away. The night brought rain squalls and heavy seas, but Sunday dawned fair. Several skates—raylike fish—were caught before noon and rigged on 14/0 hooks and wire leader. Bill Smith, a regular on the pier, again took these baits out in a small boat and dropped them well away from the pier. Only one shark had been landed all morning, an 11-foot dusky.

From time to time, a small shark picked up a bait only to drop it again. Then, Maxwell recalled, "A herd of big boys came in there."

One of them picked up the skate Maxwell was using for bait and ran with it. Apparently, that shark bit through the wire leader connecting the top hook to the bottom hook.

"It was a strong run, but I didn't hook him," Maxwell said. "I don't think it was the same shark I eventually landed because there was no hook or wire leader in its stomach when we checked later."

"In the afternoon," Michie recalled, "Nick Laney, another fisherman, hooked a big tiger about 11 feet long. We could see the stripes clearly when the fish came by the pier the first time. I was on the sand under the pier with the beached dusky when Nicky's shark bit. I scrambled back onto the pier and saw his fish. We knew he couldn't bring the fish to gaff from the pier."

Laney's 9/0 reel and 50-pound-test line were too light!

As Maxwell watched Laney's shark surging left and right and out to sea, another fish hit his own bait. The click was on but the reel was not in gear. The drag was set at about 30 pounds, pretty stiff by Maxwell's own admission.

"When he hit the bait, the shark just went out on a straight line. It was a stronger run than the one I had had on Saturday."

Suddenly the shark leaped clear of the water. The sound of the splash shocked the anglers and the spectators.

"When that fish jumped, it was only about 30 yards off the end of the pier, almost in the surf," Maxwell told me.

At about the same time, a herd of sharks hit the other baits, and some lines were broken. Then Maxwell's line was smoking out again. He had placed his rod butt in the socket of his belly plate and locked the drag on his reel. He was immediately pulled forward and down onto the pier's deck. Loosening the drag, Maxwell stumbled to his feet and tried to control the bucking rod and reel. Onlookers gasped when the giant tiger shark jumped again some 500 feet from the pier.

"There was a tremendous crashing sound, not like a king mackerel or even a sailfish," Maxwell recalled.

Was Maxwell afraid? What if the reel had seized up? Would he have been dragged into water that was evidently swarming with big sharks?

Some two decades after the event, Maxwell can afford to be calm and he insists that there was no great danger. Being dragged against the chest-high pier railing and into the water was just a remote possibility, and there was always a sharp knife handy to cut the line.

The only danger that Maxwell was concerned about was losing his second big tiger shark of the weekend. Maxwell's shark made a long run to the north and Laney's ran to the south. The fishermen had decided that the only way Laney could land his fish was to bring it to the beach well away from the pilings of the pier.

"The last time I saw Laney with the fish still on was after he had jumped from the pier onto the beach. He was running down the beach with about forty people behind him," Maxwell recalled. Laney's tiger was lost later when it charged under the pier and broke off on the pilings.

"A lot of people were coming out on the pier. Nicky's shark had already drawn a lot of people," Maxwell told me.

Maxwell's friends tried to keep the crowd at a distance by roping off the end of the pier to give him room to fight the shark.

"The water was clear, and you could see the dark stripes against the gray of its body," Maxwell remembered. "The stripes were not as distinct as they are on a smaller tiger, but they were there."

After the second jump, the fish put its head down and ran northeast, taking almost all the line out. Maxwell struggled to slow the run; Michie poured Coke bottles of water onto the overheated reel drag. The shark was more than three-quarters of a mile from the pier when Maxwell finally succeeded in bringing the fish to a gradual stop. He held it still for 30 seconds with straining arms, shoulders, and back. The man's strength was augmented by his tackle, but the shark sulked near the bottom with the huge steel hook set in its upper jaw, just outside the teeth.

Maxwell's greatest piece of luck had come when he hooked the shark at the start of the fight. If the wire leader had been inside the shark's mouth when it clamped down on the bait, its notched teeth probably would have cut through even the heavy wire leader sometime during the fight. But the lower hook had apparently been bitten off by another shark and the upper hook was embedded in the upper lip, outside the multiple rows of teeth. After the fight was over, Maxwell had to cut the hook out of the shark's lip.

"The hole that big hook made didn't enlarge at all during the long fight," Maxwell recalled.

Maxwell had to run backward and reel madly to take in line when the fish finally moved and made another fast and powerful run to the southeast. Again, luck was with the angler. When there was only a few hundred feet of line on the reel, the tiger ran parallel to the beach, toward the pier, instead of surging out to sea. Maxwell reeled as fast as was humanly possible to gather up the slack line. The fish stopped near the pier, but only for a few seconds. Again it ran, and again the line on the spool dwindled from seven inches to the diameter of a 50-cent piece. The fish came charging in again, turned, and headed away once more. Each time, Maxwell cranked the line in only to see it streak from the spool again, even though he tightened the drag cautiously. Three times the shark leaped completely clear of the water.

"On its first three runs that shark could have taken out all my line. Of course, it would have snapped," Maxwell recalled, "but the tiger seemed to want to come back to the pier to see what was up. That shark surfaced and looked over the situation.

"The fourth and fifth runs took the line down to the diameter of a silver dollar. It was about 4 P.M. by then, and the fish kept running to the northeast."

Maxwell got some relief by sitting on a high, wooden bench with his feet braced against the rail. When an angler hooks a big fish from a boat, he can sometimes set the hook and let the fish pull the boat as well as struggle against the line, and the boat can move toward the fish. Padded fighting chairs, swiveled to point the rod in the direction of the surging fish, also help a lot. But Maxwell just sat there on the hard, wooden bench. Even with the leverage of the big-game rod, his arms were weakening and he felt the effect of turning the reel handle thousands of times. His friends continued to pour water on the hot reel. Maxwell was hot, too, and very tired, but he knew that the fish was also tiring.

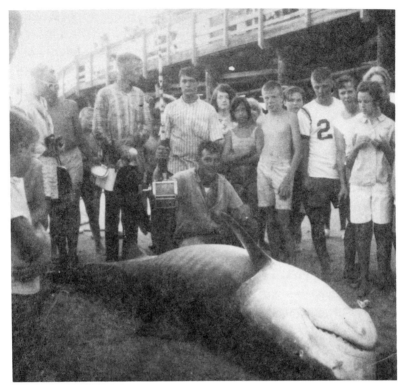

Walter Maxwell manages a smile as vacationers check out his just-caught world record tiger shark. Cherry Grove pier is in the background. The hook is still visible in the upper lip of the shark.

Photo by Jim Michie, courtesy of Walter Maxwell

Now Maxwell's in his mid-50s; he still plays softball in a local league and often belts home runs. "Here comes the old man; get the outfielders back" is what they say, according to Maxwell's own smiling testimony. Twenty years ago, on that sunny, Sunday afternoon, he was in good shape and in the prime of his strength. He knew that the shark was expending more energy than he was and that he was winning.

During the long afternoon, the shark made some 30 runs and it was clear that the tiger was losing its strength.

"He was near the pier several times," Maxwell said, "but we had gaffed a green fish the day before and had realized our mistake."

It was about half-tide when the shark was brought toward the pier for the last time. Maxwell had been fighting it for 4½ hours. He strained against the weight of the powerful fish and his heavy tackle. By now, he could see where the shark was hooked and he took advantage of the lip hook-up to pull the huge mouth open.

The gaff that Michie held in his hands differed from the one that had been wrenched from his grip the previous day. This gaff hook was also attached to a fiberglass pole but, in addition, a rope was tied to the eye of the gaff in case the pole broke or was wrenched away.

Michie wanted to gaff the fish inside the mouth. As he put it, "A big fish like that gaffed in the dorsal area or in the body can tear loose from the gaff."

Michie struck with the gaff, and the shark brought its primitive forces into play again and tried to surge away. The pole pulled out of the gaff hook and Maxwell's friends pulled tight on the rope.

"Once that shark was gaffed, he was caught," Michie told me. "Jim waded out beneath the pier and put a head rope and a tail rope on him and we dragged him onto the sand."

Jim Michie was the first to say it: "There's no doubt—that's a record."

It was after 6 P.M. A wrecker was called to lift the fish up onto a flatbed truck. Bushels of shrimp and what seemed like barrels of seawater and half-digested food spewed up from the maw of the shark. The fish was already beginning to lose weight and the company of shark anglers still had to truck the fish to a scale big enough to weigh it.

It was not until 9 A.M. on the following day that the fish was weighed on the government-certified truck scale at Ford's Fuel Service in Loris, South Carolina. The temperature had been in the 80s late Sunday afternoon, and dehydration overnight probably took at least 10 percent of the shark's weight, in addition to the weight lost with the stomach contents. Even so, notary public Jessie Ruth Graham attested to a weight of 1,780 pounds, a girth of 103 inches, and a length of 13 feet 10.5 inches.

Maxwell's tiger shark weighed 350 pounds more than the previous IGFA all-tackle record. Allowing for dehydration overnight and the loss of the stomach contents, it is very likely that Maxwell had been battling a shark that weighed more than a ton. And he caught the monster shark from a pier, a feat unmatched in the entire history of big-game fishing.

Part Two:

Fishermen and Fishing Places

Introduction

Any place a boat can be docked or launched, in fact, any island or inlet or stretch of beach or fishing pier from Cape Lookout and Beaufort Inlet in North Carolina, past South Carolina's Cape Romain and Charleston's jetties to Georgia's Sapelo Island and Altamaha Sound could provide enough fishing for a lifetime. The fishermen (always understand that some of the best and most devoted of them are women) are themselves the potential source of a wealth of experience for anyone who has eyes to see and ears to hear their stories. With the following chapters I can only hope to touch the riches the Southeast coast presents through its fishermen and fishing places. The note of melancholy that will be heard in the words of many of the older fishermen is balanced by the echoes of a beauty and abundance that still linger. What I wish for all those who share this experience with me is not only the eyes to see and the ears to hear but the will to speak in defense of this coastal heritage.

17

North Carolina

Morehead City: "We Average Out Right Well"

The chamber of commerce calls it North Carolina's "Crystal Coast": to the east and north the long barrier island of Cape Lookout National Seashore, the sheltered waters behind it (think flounder and trout, spot, croaker, and small blues) lapping at the shore of "maritime" Carteret County, and to the south, burgeoning with new condominiums scattered between old fishing piers, the more accessible but storm-vulnerable strip of sand and scrub growth called the Bogue Banks. At the center of this world permeated with the clean smell of saltwater is the port of Morehead City, home to hundreds of sport and commercial fishing boats. It is well worth a trip to the docks anytime, but especially late on a deliciously clear Saturday afternoon in mid-autumn.

First boat in is the "Carolina Princess," two hours early because, as the dockmaster put it, "There just wasn't any more room for fish." Captain "Woo Woo" Harker has taken his 65-foot headboat and 70 passengers for an easy day of snapper bank fishing in only 110 feet of water. (The farther you have to drop your bait, the longer you have to reel up your fish—or your cleaned hooks. Go bottom fishing in 30 fathoms and crank in a pound or so of lead sinker or, better still, a five-pound trigger fish turning its flat body against the water and feeling like a manhole cover; suddenly, an electric reel doesn't seem as unsporting a proposition.)

The captain slides his boat neatly into its berth which sports a "Woo Woo For President Headquarters" sign, no doubt inspired

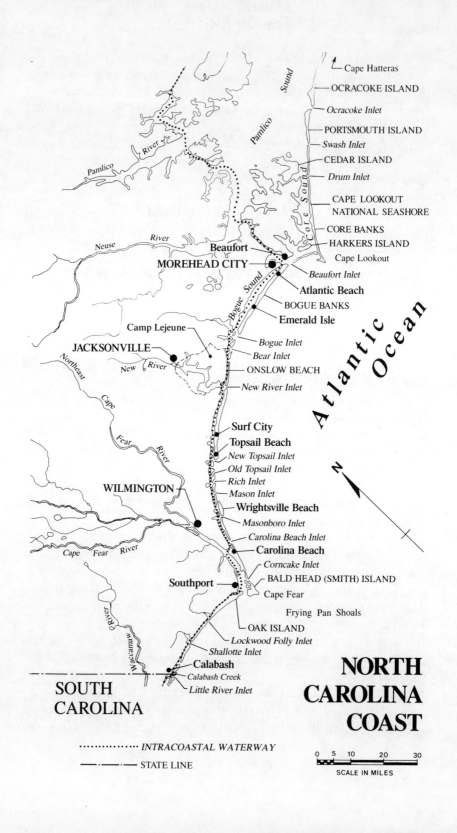

Cape Hatteras

—OCRACOKE ISLAND

Ocracoke Inlet

—PORTSMOUTH ISLAND

Swash Inlet

—CEDAR ISLAND

Drum Inlet

CAPE LOOKOUT
NATIONAL SEASHORE

—CORE BANKS

—HARKERS ISLAND

Cape Lookout

Pamlico Sound

Pamlico River

Pamlico

Core Sound

Beaufort

MOREHEAD CITY

Neuse River

Beaufort Inlet

Atlantic Beach

BOGUE BANKS

Bogue Sound

Emerald Isle

Camp Lejeune

JACKSONVILLE

Bogue Inlet

Bear Inlet

New River

—ONSLOW BEACH

New River Inlet

Northeast

Surf City

Topsail Beach

New Topsail Inlet

Cape

Old Topsail Inlet

Rich Inlet

Fear River

Mason Inlet

WILMINGTON

Wrightsville Beach

Masonboro Inlet

Carolina Beach Inlet

Carolina Beach

Cape Fear River

Corncake Inlet

Southport

BALD HEAD (SMITH) ISLAND

Cape Fear

Frying Pan Shoals

Atlantic Ocean

N

OAK ISLAND

Lockwood Folly Inlet

Shallotte Inlet

River

Calabash

Calabash Creek

Waccamaw

Little River Inlet

**SOUTH
CAROLINA**

NORTH
CAROLINA
COAST

·············· *INTRACOASTAL WATERWAY*

—··— STATE LINE

0 5 10   20   30

SCALE IN MILES

by a boatload of successful anglers. This day's catch will perhaps move him up in the polls. To the newcomer, it may appear at first glance that hanging from the upper deck of the husky wood headboat are bulky, glistening bundles of fruit. Of course, what's there are stringers of fish, hung on rough hemp and swaying as the boat slides into its berth. (The fish have been taken from the boat's coolers, just before docking, and hung up as a sort of advertisement to lure future customers.) Grouper, grouper, grouper, olive and brown and tan, and mixed in are bright vermilion snapper, angular drab triggerfish, and silver snapper, the hint of pink explaining their other name, "pink porgy." It has indeed been a fruitful day of fishing just a two-hour run offshore.

Offshore for the Morehead City fleet is the last best part of reef fishing on the south Atlantic coast. North of Morehead City few Carolina headboats brave the less predictable Atlantic, the waters of Cape Hatteras being more hospitable to surfcasters (who are not stopped by rough seas) and to smaller and faster sportfishing boats, whose skippers can pick and choose their fishing days. Morehead City also happens to be more easily accessible to the one-day fisherman willing to rise early in the morning (or drive all night from Atlanta or Washington or even Philadelphia). And because the further north one moves up the Southeast coast, the more stormy and foreboding the weather possibilities, the offshore reefs here have been spared some of the pressure of commercial fishing (hook and line, traps, and trawlers with huge nets) that have taken a big bite out of offshore bottomfish populations further south. "Probatur agendo," as the Latin translation of the Greek proverb goes: the proof is in the stringers at Morehead City, and heavy with grouper they are on this golden fall afternoon.

A tall young mate—his features those of one of the male stars of the TV soaps but with the rugged complexion of a man working for a living at sea—wearing foul weather gear only in preparation for scrubbing down his fish-stained "Carolina Princess" lines up his passengers on the dock and with a courtesy almost exaggerated but in no way condescending dispenses their stringers of fish. The captain is busy helping lug a recently purchased anchor to the bow of his headboat. The huge hook is rusty, obviously old, and serviceable, a piece of gear perfectly suited to his old workhorse "Princess." (By the fall of 1986, a brand new "Carolina Princess" had replaced its namesake with the wooden hull and the ancient anchor.) On leave from nearby Camp Lejeune, a young marine, the sides of his head shaved well above his ears, surveys the catch. He wants to go to sea to fish in the morning and I remember my first weekend pass from Fort Bragg and a trip to a coastal Carolina pier a quarter of a century ago. The lure of fishing is always strong for a young man who loves the sea.

His boat backed into the dock between other boats and among fish houses, gift shops, and restaurants, Captain Leroy Gould climbs ashore from the "Mattie G II" after putting in another day of his thirty-fifth year at the helm of a Morehead City fishing boat. "We still have good fishing here, no problem about that," he says. "We have better boats, faster boats, and with the way some fish are spread out we need those boats. We have to cover more distance to get the same amount of fish we once caught." Gould's wife is sitting on a park-type bench thoughtfully provided by the city. The dock area is pleasantly clean and the soft day doesn't yet require a sweater even though the sun is sinking behind the docked boats. The woman smiles at her husband's comment that his 23-year-old boat may last longer than its captain.

Captain Gould is concerned about coastal Carolina offshore fishing. "Fish used to stay in an area longer. We could catch bottomfish such as snapper—they were in abundance because you didn't have as many fishermen—vee-liners (vermilions) on up to American (snappers) in 100 to 110 feet of water. They were a whole lot more plentiful than they are now. . . . They've over-fished with traps and with lines, too."

"Nature decides on a particular day's fishing," Gould says as he describes an average trip. "You have your currents, you got your tides, and you may get over the fish. . . . We have machines to tell us when we're over the fish, but we haven't had a machine to make 'em bite. You have fair days, you have good days, and you have some sorry days. We average out quite well and that's what brings our groups back. They manage to have a nice time each trip."

The captain's words are borne out by Dr. Gene Huntsman of the National Marine Fisheries Service (NMFS) in nearby Beau-

A mixed catch of snapper and grouper on the "Carolina Princess" out of Morehead City

fort. A survey of catches on South Atlantic headboats conducted by NMFS since 1972 has shown that the best catches between the Florida Keys and Cape Lookout, North Carolina, are made in this northernmost area of the survey. An average of 25 pounds per angler per day was reported in a recent year for the waters off Morehead City, with the catch rate declining almost uniformly southward along the coast to under 8 pounds per angler per day off Key West.

Captain Gould is not happy about two things, porpoises and trawlers, "draggers" as he calls them. "If you don't watch out they're going to have to thin these porpoises out. . . . There's nothing thinning porpoises out. Can you imagine how many fish a hungry porpoise eats a day?" The commercial trawlers that drag the inshore waters in spring and fall are also hurting fishing, notes Gould. "Your bass multiplies in here," he says gesturing toward the sheltered waters of the coast, nursery to juvenile fish of hundreds of species. The connection between the survival of juvenile channel bass and the survival of gamefishing on the coast is not lost on this veteran fisherman.

The sun's last rays are being filtered through the windows of a commercial fishing boat moored stern in toward the bulkhead. We approach a display of seashells surrounding a booth marked "Capt. Stacy IV." Seated behind a desk to the side of a popcorn machine and presiding over telephones, a gift shop, and bookings for sportfishing boats is Loretta, the smiling blonde daughter of Captain Sonny Davis, himself a fisherman's son. Her brother is off for a few days and her father is running the boat today, an easy trip with 46 fishermen on a company charter, plenty of elbow room on what the Davises proudly advertise as "The Brand New 83' x 22', 1800 H.P. Super Head Boat."

In the twilight, the stringers of vermilion snapper stand out aglow, bunch after tapered bunch decorating both port and starboard of the sparkling white fiberglass boat. It is still almost three weeks to Thanksgiving, but it is as if the coast were anticipating Christmas decorations the only way it knew how. Here and there a trigger fish sets off the colorful snapper and a stringer of grouper shows that the crew had time to fish, too.

The captain's white locks belie his 45 years. A thin waist and a hard, lean muscular frame show that he not only works hard but takes care to stay in shape, not always an easy task when one's workday is 12 hours at sea. "Fishing has changed quite a bit," he admits. "We have gone to faster boats and more modern equipment so catches have held up. The last five years we've caught more vermilions than ever. Two drops and you filled the boat five years ago and lots of grouper and porgies, silver snapper, too."

Today's catch is still impressive, but will people be able to enjoy such fishing 20 or 30 years from now? "I don't believe so; I don't know how they can." This captain has another complaint: "Loran C (a navigation system that allows a skipper to find an exact spot of ocean bottom that he had the "numbers" for) has hurt fishing more than anything else, because it makes fishermen out of weekenders." He tells of a 24-foot boat that followed him out this day. "Once he gets on the spot he can get back . . . they get the numbers and all they have to do is push the numbers in and they're gone. The skill part of it is just about gone."

He talks about learning to fish off the Florida coast in the late 1950s, of using buoys to mark the bottom, and learning what the bottom was like and how to find the fish. With Loran, the machine gets the fisherman back to that great offshore reef. He says it again: "Loran C has hurt fishing more than anything else."

Most fishermen are not above an ironic view of themselves and their vocation. Davis chuckles as he tells about being the first skipper to run Gulf Stream headboat trips from Morehead City in the 1960s. "It was a 47-foot headboat called the 'Tradewinds' and Captain Frank Juel (from Little River, South Carolina) bought it from me later. We would bring in a boatload of grouper and people would ask 'What are they? Are they good to eat?' Groupers have come up the hill quite a bit since that time." He smiles and tells of shipping 1,000 pounds of grouper on consignment to the Fulton Fish Market in New York. No one bought them. "I got a bill for freight on them."

As we talk, the crew of the "Captain Stacy IV" is scrubbing the boat from top to waterline. It is dark and only one fine stringer of vermilions still lies on the dock, no longer illuminated by the natural light of day but by the glare of the headboat's deck lights. The stringer is the subject of discussion between two members of the crew and the captain. "You got my fish," someone says, mostly in jest. This is the next to last weekend of a season which will end before Thanksgiving.

"In April we start sailing again," Captain Davis adds, "five days a week. We get lots of charters." Before one season is over, the fisherman is looking forward to the next.

The Bogue Banks:
"In Numbers Unequaled Anywhere Else Along Our Coast"

Our title is the way Dr. Robert J. Goldstein describes the pier fishing of the Bogue Banks in his comprehensive work *Pier Fishing in North Carolina* published in 1978. Goldstein, an avid pier fisherman who is just as much at home offshore after yellowfin tuna, goes on to note that it seems at times as if fish "piled up below the bight of Cape Lookout." I thought of this knowledgeable North Carolina writer and fisherman as I soaked up the afternoon sun and the salty atmosphere on the Emerald Isle Pier on a recent fall afternoon. It was just as he had described it.

The temperature had fallen into the high 30's overnight, our first cool spell of the autumn coming after a week of muggy, rainy weather. When the rains had passed, severe flooding had occurred inland in the Carolinas and even worse in Virginia, but the only effect on the coast was to scrub it clean, water and air, and stir the appetites of fish and fishermen. With just a slight chop on the water thanks to a gentle wind from the west, hundreds of anglers were out on the pier for a day of bottom fishing. Some were still wearing their skimobile suits that make fishing on a chilly morning tolerable. Most had gone to light jackets and sweaters, but their pails and coolers had evidence that the waters were still warm. Flounder (fluke to Northerners, a big-mouthed fish, not the small sucker of worms and clams) had been hitting one after another. One angler displayed two fish that weighed, in total, at least 10 pounds and there were few summer flounder under 2 pounds.

It was a good day for those fishing near the surf for flatfish. Farther out on the pier there were mixed catches of trout and

Pierfishing for big flounder often results in good catches on the Bogue Banks.

saltwater panfish, pigfish and spot being the fish most consistently pulled over the side. It seemed that everybody had caught some fish, even two young men who had quite obviously been drinking more than moderately as they waited for a bite. Skates and sea mullet (whiting) were being caught, the latter treated more kindly, although the skate would have once made a fine bait for giant sharks. (Sharkfishing, which has produced some record fish for Carolina pier anglers, has almost disappeared as a pier-fishing pursuit in recent years because, say some pier owners, it keeps many other anglers from their less hazardous and disruptive pursuits. One shark fisherman insists it's strictly an economic issue: Ten spot anglers spend more than ten times what one shark angler would spend in the pier tackle-and-snack shop. Shark fishermen are never shoulder-to-shoulder along the rail as sometimes occurs when spot, bluefish, or trout are running and anglers jam the piers.)

The kings have gone out to sea and south for the year, but at pier after pier that afternoon we see the chalkboards covered with records of big king mackerel taken from June through September. But there are cobia and tarpon listed, too, and Spanish mackerel and big bluefish, spotted sea trout and gray trout, and every variety of bottom feeder from sea mullet (whiting) to croaker. On one of the piers an angler is cleaning a bonito taken on a jig and feather rig, while another young fisherman casts to what looked like a 20-pound bluefish that had just broken water under a school of baitfish.

On the beach, there are more anglers, fishing with cut bait for flounder and blues. Most have brought folding chairs in which to relax. White sandspikes made of plastic pipe are used to hold the rods, while the fishermen watch their rod tips silhouetted against the blue sky for that sudden dip toward the surf that indicates a bite. Behind the leisurely anglers there is a grim reminder, a tangible notice that man is there at nature's sufferance, for on the dunes there lies evidence of the passage of Hurricane Diana earlier in the fall, pilings and boards from what was the end of Sportsman's Pier. But repairs have been made where possible and damaged sections roped off. The fishermen of the Bogue Banks need their piers, always at the mercy of a stormy Atlantic, but a pleasant and productive place to be on an autumn day made just for fishing.

Topsail Island: Wading for Trout

From New River Inlet on the north to Topsail Inlet on the south, from piers with such romantic names as Barnacle Bill's and the Scotch Bonnet, from the surf at Surf City and from holes all along the beach, dedicated fishermen like Rick Forgach find Topsail Island a fine place to fish for spotted sea trout, particularly in the fall. While others are taking their trout and flounder in New River Inlet, Forgach concentrates much of his fishing on the ocean side of the island.

When he's not fishing for trout and flounder, two of his favorite species, Rick presides over an emporium dedicated to the average fisherman with above-average determination. It's called "Rick's Place," on N.C. Highway 210 East within an easy drive of some of the best spotted sea trout fishing on the North Carolina coast—when the fish are biting. If you need a bag of really fresh shrimp to fish under a float for trout, or just want to hear where the fish were hitting yesterday or this morning, stop in to see Rick. He's liable to open a cooler and show you a six-pound spotted sea trout just to whet your appetite.

Rick fishes with grubs and Mirrolures, the 54M Mirrolure with fluorescent head and yellow body being one of his favorites. His two-handed spinning rod and medium-size reel enable him to flip that plug far out into the incoming tide at both ends of Topsail Island: New River Inlet and Topsail Inlet. "Just before and just after high tide is best," Rick notes. Watch him as he casts and retrieves with a slow, steady turn on the reel and an occasional flip of the rod, often followed by a strike that in no uncertain terms announces that the trout are in.

Anywhere along the beach that there are holes may be the place to fish, Rick points out. Investigate the beach at low tide and come back to fish the incoming tide all the way up to high tide. North of the Surf City pier and near the location of the old Paradise Pier are two good places for the first-time trout fisherman to try. On those chilly November mornings when the water temperature has finally gone below 60 degrees and the air temperature may be down in the 30's, Rick pulls his waders over his warmest fishing clothes and heads for the ocean.

Rick Forgach shows why fishermen gather at his place for bait and information. The spotted sea trout hit a "Mirrolure" plug fished in the surf.

In addition to the Mirrolure plugs, he also touts the Mister Twister in green or white as a top trout lure. He has taken up to 30 trout on one trip, but a quarter of that number would satisfy most spotted sea trout anglers. Rick also likes to fish for trout from the piers at night. "I remember one December night when it was calm I went out on Barnacle Bill's at 9 P.M. and fished around the high tide. I think I ended up with about 15 trout and the average was over three pounds." One or two of those would make my day—or night.

Pier fishing on Topsail Island is highlighted by croaker and spot in early spring, with flounder running from April through November. King mackerel are taken on trolley-line rigs beginning in May and will continue through early fall. September is a super time to try, weather permitting. Good Spanish mackerel fishing is sometimes found in the summer months, but no matter how good the rest of it is, Rich Forgach still loves his winter trout.

Wilmington: Easy Surfcasting and a Civil War Legacy

The traditional image of surfcasting is of someone the size of John Wayne swathed in chest-high waders, with perhaps a hooded slicker top to match, wading out of a pounding surf that shows white water to the horizon. In one hand is a channel bass that weighs 40 pounds, or perhaps a bluefish of half that size. This rugged angler, for only a real man or a very tough woman could fish such a surf, is holding in the other hand a huge spinning rod that could well be used as an emergency telegraph pole, rarely under 12 feet in length. Attached to the rod, preferably with tape rather than a reel seat—another indication of the angler's professional dedications—is a reel that looks as if it could hold 400 yards of 20-pound test monofilament. Like so many other false images, this one really doesn't work for most of the North Carolina surf from the Bogue Banks down through Surf City to Cape Fear and down to Shallotte Inlet. Professor John Scalf of the University of North Carolina's Wilmington campus will testify to this and give us a history lesson in the bargain.

The fact is that the surf along the southern coast of North Carolina down through South Carolina and on to the Georgia Sea Islands is not as mean nor as huge as it is off the Outer Banks and on northward. It may be rough at times, but there are also days when freshwater spinning tackle is ideal for fishing. Aside from the beaches at the edge of inlets when the tide is in mid-course, forget the big poles, forget the waders, forget the reels the size of bowling balls. Think medium tackle, smaller lures, and some of the easiest surf fishing on the Atlantic coast.

"My favorite fishing in springtime," Dr. Scalf notes, "is to search the surf for the early runs of Virginia mullet (whiting or sea mullet). They show up in the beach depressions which are underwater valleys in the sand created by run-offs and tides." His favorite holes include one in front of the Sheraton Hotel at Wrightsville Beach and another just above the Northern Extension Pier at Carolina Beach. He also likes the rocks at Fort Fisher. "Almost any type rod and reel will suffice with a simple terminal tackle rigged with number 6 hooks baited with cut mullet, shrimp, or sand fleas." In the fall the same areas will yield an abundance of small bluefish, with the lightest of saltwater spinning outfits perfectly suited to the small blues.

When the fish won't come to the beach, Scalf goes to the fish: slow trolling for king mackerel in the late spring and early fall off Cape Fear and the beaches or drifting for flounder in the summer in Masonboro Inlet, Rich's Inlet, Mason's Inlet, or Old Topsail Inlet are all productive. But the king is the thing that excites anticipation: "The fall is the expected harvest of the year," the genial and learned professor notes, "and the Wrightsville Beach King Mackerel Tournament is our premier event."

With a professor's eye to educating his listeners, Scalf adds that one of the greatest resources of the Cape Fear area is a relic of the Civil War. "Wilmington was the last port open to the Confederacy. . . . The attempts to supply the Confederacy and Union efforts to stymie this flow resulted in the sinking of some 40 Civil War ships, from North and South, that remain in our waters. . . . Charter boats have been carrying customers to these areas since the 1930s." Today an armada of private craft still fish

Professor John Scalf, center, aids Dr. Richard Moore in measuring and tagging a black sea bass caught by Randy Nimmons of Coastal Carolina College. Scalf's student anglers of the University of North Carolina–Wilmington have won the intercollegiate world championship four times.

these "trout holes," often unaware that the "hole" that produced a cooler full of gray trout is part of the legacy of the War Between the States. Scalf again recommends light tackle. "Cut bait or shrimp is all that's needed. My favorite spots are over the U.S.S. *Peterhoff* at the mouth of Corncake Inlet or the *Condor* in front of the monument at Fort Fisher."

In the winter, the good professor just dresses for the weather and heads for the river off downtown Wilmington. "One of the best-kept secrets of the local fishing fraternity," he reveals, "has been the presence of stripers wintering in the river within sight of the city lights. The fish hang around the piers from the North Carolina State Ports docking areas north to where the Cape Fear River and Northeast Cape Fear River come together . . . Five-pound stripers are regularly caught there, but 20 to 25 pounders are not uncommon . . . . Point Peter, just across the river from the Hilton Hotel, is my favorite spot."

What Dr. Scalf does not mention is that his student anglers from U.N.C.-Wilmington have often won what amounts to the world championship of intercollegiate angling, the Coastal Carolina Invitational, usually with a co-ed team. Coach Scalf has also been as gracious in defeat as he has been magnanimous in victory in the Invitationals which combine competitive fishing with seminars on the environment and the future of sportfishing. For those who want to learn more about fishing the North Carolina coast (you will note that the good professor kept mum about his favorite spots for sheepshead and spotted sea trout), a trip to Springmaid Beach at the end of September when the Invitational is held may provide the opportunity for more detailed questioning of the learned doctor about fishing the waters near his home on the North Carolina coast.

Bald Head Island: The Professionals

In Section VI of the *Anglers' Guide to the United States Atlantic Coast*, published by the U.S. Department of Commerce and the National Marine Fisheries Service in 1976, the fishing map of the North Carolina–South Carolina border area centers on Cape Fear and Smith Island. But look at the color aerial photos of the same island in magazine or newspaper advertising and editorial copy covering the development of the southern coast of North Carolina and you will see nary a reference to Smith Island. This wedge of sand dunes, marsh, creeks, and ponds has been transmuted into a resort, Bald Head Island, and it is home to some of the most competitive young fishermen on the coast, two boys named Tom who know how to catch kings for money, as well as cobia, trout, and flounder for fun and the table.

Tom Plankers is the head professional at the Bald Head Island golf course (try it from the championship tees on a windy day in early spring if you think you're a golfer!), and Tommy Dosher is a foreman with the building and grounds section of the resort. Both would rather fish, and they do it very professionally.

Anyone who works or lives at Bald Head has a great place to start for North Carolina coastal fishing. Sitting like a wedge at the entrance to the Cape Fear River, Bald Head Island and its protected marina provide easy access not only to estuary fishing for flounder and trout, both gray and speckled, but to bigger game as well. Off East Beach there are big red drum in the fall. Given the right weather, a small boat with a hardy crew can be into yellowfin tuna, billfish, and dolphin in under three hours. Around Frying Pan Shoals, which is not a long run offshore, a few sailfish are taken late every summer as these spectacular billfish move in to compete with the kings for a late-season feast of baitfish around Lighthouse Rock, just a dozen miles or so offshore.

It is the menhaden that are the bread and butter of the young pros' larder, the live bait that whether fished out near the Gulf Stream or just offshore from Oak Island down to Little River Inlet, have turned king mackerel fishing into a young man's game. In their game plan, Dosher and Plankers are always looking for bait for starters. Because of their duties, each is on a different schedule, Plankers in a 24-foot Grady White, Dosher in a commercial boat with center console that he has converted to the perfect live-bait fishing machine. When the kings are running, the young pros can't wait to get at them. But first the live bait.

As I cruised with Dosher one windy afternoon we searched the waters off Oak Island for any sign of menhaden. A brown streak in the already murky water gave them away—flipping tails and a dark shadowmass of fish breaking the water are another eagerly awaited cue—and it took just one throw of a huge casting net to bring a hundred or so "perfect" baits into the boat. The menhaden are immediately placed in a transparent barrellike holding tank with seawater constantly circulating through a pump system which is essential to this kind of fishing.

"We can keep most of our baits alive for a three-hour trip offshore," Dosher assured me. Instead of trying to fool billfish and tuna with artificials, he and his fishing companions ("My wife loves to fish," Dosher noted) are able to put frisky live baits on light tackle in front of sometimes finicky gamefish. The results are spectacular. Anyone who has ever had two or three trolled lures or live baits attacked by a trio of yellowfin or bull dolphin or wahoo or kings will never forget the experience. For a pro like Dosher, it's business as usual, but he is not afraid to share his secrets, even with competitors who may be entering the same big money king mackerel tournaments that he's fishing. The only drawback to fishing with him is that he wants to set every hook himself. That's the sign of the tournament king fisher in him.

One of his secrets is hard work. He and his father have constructed a live-bait holding tank at his mainland home, just across the Cape Fear River from Bald Head. The day and sometimes the night before a big fishing trip, especially during a tournament, is devoted to making sure that there is live bait aplenty. Painstaking care with tackle is another. Light, coffee-colored wire leaders that are tied by twisting rather than with crimps, two or three treble hooks painted with marine paint to eliminate any metal flash, light monofilament line in mint condition—20-pound-test is plenty for kings—are the mainstays of his fishing arsenal.

Six baits, some fished deep by way of downriggers with quick release clips, some held away from the boat with outriggers, all swimming at their proper distances and rarely tangling—this is the game plan of the professional angler. According to Plankers, the careful light-wire king rig should never fail the angler.

When the weather isn't right or the kings aren't in or there just isn't enough time away from the job, where do the Bald Head Island pros go? To the creeks and sheltered waters for flounder and trout, and to the beach for big red drum. Plankers will even brave the chill of a November night to fish with cut bait for drum, with 30 pounders not unusual. Dosher makes up his own double hook flounder rigs designed to foil the flatfish that hits a strip bait short. Nothing, or at least as little as possible, is left to chance by these professionals.

When I asked another Bald Head Island fishing fanatic, Jim Hart, executive director of the Carolinas PGA, what he liked about the island besides its spectacular golf course, his answer was "the bluefish in the surf." You can tell that Hart's not a fishing professional. But even the amateurs have fun at Bald Head Island—or just offshore. If you don't believe me, ask the professionals.

Southport: North Carolina's Great Communicator

Take an informal poll of fishermen east of the Mississippi and north of the Sun Belt. Ask them which state on the East Coast has the best and most varied saltwater fishing opportunities. The odds are in favor of North Carolina, in part because of its natural resources, in part due to the tireless promotion of a former A.C.C. football hero, Joel Arrington. Arrington not only promotes North Carolina fishing, but he fishes energetically and often innovatively.

A charter boat skipper from Southport was excited at the prospect of a big cobia for show-and-tell back at the dock. Arrington was bringing the fish to the gaff over one of North Carolina's many artificial reefs. The skipper noted that not since the last time Arrington had fished on his boat had anyone taken a cobia like that from the reef. "Of course," Arrington later pointed out, "nobody had tried jigging for them with this skipper since the last time I had been out with him." (A jigged lure is bounced up and down, either just off the bottom, or in mid water; raised rapidly by a lift of the rod tip, the lure flutters down like an injured baitfish.) Nobody had been innovative enough to rig a spinning rod with a heavy bucktail jig that could be used to excite cobia, kings, and amberjack to bite even in the presence of an abundance of natural bait. But Arrington had done it, much to the delight of the outdoor writers and photographers from around the country whom he so frequently hosted during his years with the North Carolina Division of Travel and Tourism.

Arrington also knows when to quit, as I discovered one day

Joel Arrington was the guide for a reef-jigging expedition that yielded this grouper.

Photo by Joel Arrington, courtesy of the N.C. Division of Travel and Tourism

on a trip out of Southport. The water was murky, so he suggested we knock off after we found that only a few seabass and a "slippery cod" were to be jigged up on one of the inshore reefs. "You break your back jigging and all that's down there are some small seabass." We headed for cleaner water further offshore, but when the winds picked up he knew when to call it a day. There would be other days on the North Carolina reefs.

The use of slow-trolling techniques for kings has dramatically changed the big-money king mackerel tournaments held from ports such as Southport. What used to be in good part a matter of luck—would the biggest king happen to hit your trolled spoon or rigged bait?—has become a match dominated by anglers versed in the art of slow trolling live baits, most often menhaden, with light tackle. Arrington has introduced writers from as far away as New England and New York to this technique as practiced by the youthful fishermen of Southport and Bald Head Island. While I had managed one king by slow trolling in my own little boat before Arrington set me up on a trip with Captain J.R. Thompson, my seminar on the water not only produced three

Captain J.R. Thompson throws a big net for menhaden to be used as live bait for king mackerel fishing. Anglers from Southport, North Carolina, helped to popularize slow-trolling techniques for kings.

big kings and a hammerhead shark, but it also served as a practical class in how to slow troll my own live baits.

What had been a mystery to older charter boat skippers fishing the coasts of North Carolina and South Carolina—leaping kings that would not hit spoons, strip baits, or ballyhoo—became a source of strike after strike, once Arrington's friends showed us how to do it with slow trolled live baits on the lightest of wire leaders and light saltwater tackle. Sharing information and spreading the gospel of his state's sportfishing resources come easy to this truly great communicator of North Carolina angling.

Calabash: Big Red Snapper—"A Thing of the Past"

"Goodnight, Mrs. Calabash, wherever you are." When I heard Jimmy Durante signing off with this line on his radio programs back before the age of television, I did not anticipate enjoying an occasional delightful seafood dinner in the tiny North Carolina waterfront village that had such pleasant memories, according to the conjectures of some pop culture historians, for one of my favorite comedians. Captain Jimmy Stevens and his headboat, the "Capt. Jim," are still creating memories of Calabash. His own memory of fishing the Carolina coast goes back a long way, too.

You can find Captain Stevens up early any summer morning at his boatdock on the waterfront. He's getting ready for another half day of black seabass fishing for customers who may have just gone for a cruise with him the night before after a dinner of light-batter fried Calabash seafood. They'll all catch fish if the weather is good. If it isn't, the captain will probably stay at the dock. It's a good time to talk to this man who has spent the last 50 years fishing the Carolina coast.

Stevens bought his first boat in 1949 and he has had a dozen since, including a succession of "Capt. Jim's," "Capt. Jim's Bonito's," and the "Bonito." The first "Captain Jim's Bonito" is probably the most interesting boat of the series, however. Stevens specialized in buying old boats, reconditioning them, running them for a year or two to prove their renewed seaworthiness, and then selling them, often promising to retire. Retirement never lasted more than a month, because once he got caught up with all the home repairs his energetic and equally hard-working

Captain Jimmy Stevens heads for the dock with one of his famous fishing boats.

wife, Juanita, wanted done, he would buy another boat and go through the process again.

What made the first "Capt. Jim's Bonito" unique was that it had been the worst hard-luck boat on the Southeast coast before Stevens bought it. How many fishermen have cold, queasy memories of trips out of Murrells Inlet aboard the old "Flying Fisher II" on a dreary, windy, rainy fall day that eventually found them some 40 miles out in the ocean and dead in the water? More than once the old boat had to be towed to port, prompting some to suggest that it be turned into an artificial reef. Not Captain Jimmy Stevens. He turned that old boat, through thousands of hours of hard work, into a hard-working headboat. Skinned knuckles, bumps on the head, even broken bones went with the territory of a man who was convinced that hard work on boat maintenance and repair would do wonders: engine, electrical, even structural repairs, all done right even if it took staying up until dawn to finish the previous day's work.

Hard work in the captain's seat was what allowed Stevens to survive over five decades of a business that could be best described as precarious. When he skippered the "Carolina Princess" for Charley Strickland in the early 1970s there was one summer when he ran 44 days in a row, June 1 to July 14. He spent most of that decade fighting for business in Little River, South Carolina, just over the border from Calabash. There were headboat wars on occasion: cars full of tourists heading for a day of fishing were met by the mates from the various boats trying to steer customers their way for the day. Stevens had enough of it and headed north to Calabash. (Another skipper, Captain Steve Speros, would move his headboat south to Vereen's Marina in North Myrtle Beach.)

When I first fished with Stevens in the mid-1970s he was specializing in all-day trips to the Gulf Stream. I recall one trip with a happy charter group from Holly Farms Chicken in North Carolina. Youngsters on down to 12 years old were catching lots of silver snapper and a few grouper and red snapper. A stringer of fish that one young man had trouble dragging off the boat stands out in my memory. But the decline had started already and Stevens noticed how fishing was changing. "Long lines run along a ledge with cut bait were getting all the big fish. Things just kept going downhill. Big reds are a thing of the past and there will never again be big grouper. There's just too much commercial fishing out there. It got to where I couldn't produce and satisfy my customers, so I went to half-day trips for blackfish. But even the blackfish are petering out. The trappers did it."

Does he still run any full-day trips out toward the Gulf Stream? "Once a year I carry people from the campground," he admits. His voice brightens. "I have a spot out there I hadn't fished in a while. We got 30 groupers in 20 minutes." Not everything is slower, he adds. "We used to didn't have the vee-liners (vermilion snapper); now they've moved down here."

Before or after that next seafood dinner at Calabash, why not say hello to Captain Jimmy Stevens down at the waterfront? You might find him still working on his boat after running it all day.

18
South Carolina

Little River: George Washington Could Have Fished Here

As I maneuver my small boat in search of a spotted sea trout or spottail bass hungry enough to hit a bright green twister-tail lure, a mist rises in the distance from the surf breaking on the shore next to the rock jetties at the mouth of Little River Inlet. The jetties are a good example of the cooperation of two states and the federal government to ensure that commercial and recreational fishermen have access to Calabash Creek, the Little River, and the Intracoastal Waterway here at the southeastern terminus of the border between North Carolina and South Carolina.

When George Washington enjoyed the hospitality of Little River on his first southern tour after his election to the presidency of the newly created United States of America, there was good fishing anyplace offshore for black seabass. (I should note that Washington's interest in fishing was not just recreational but economic: His Mount Vernon plantation often derived more of its annual income from net-fishing in the Potomac than from farming!) Some 150 years later, with our country in the midst of the Great Depression, Captain Frank Juel recalls that "anyone could take a hundred pounds of blackfish in an easy day's fishing." The fishing's not that good anymore, but, thanks to the jetties, both commercial and sportfishermen have a little easier time getting to their livelihood and recreation out of Little River Inlet.

During the 1930s young Frank Juel worked for 50 cents a day on the headboat "Josephine." (His father was a member of the crew and earned $2.50 a day, Juel recalls.) "The fare for passengers was just a dollar. I was eleven years old and back then we fished in sight of land and caught blackfish pretty much anywhere we fished. It was no trick for someone to take a hundred pounds of fish on a handline."

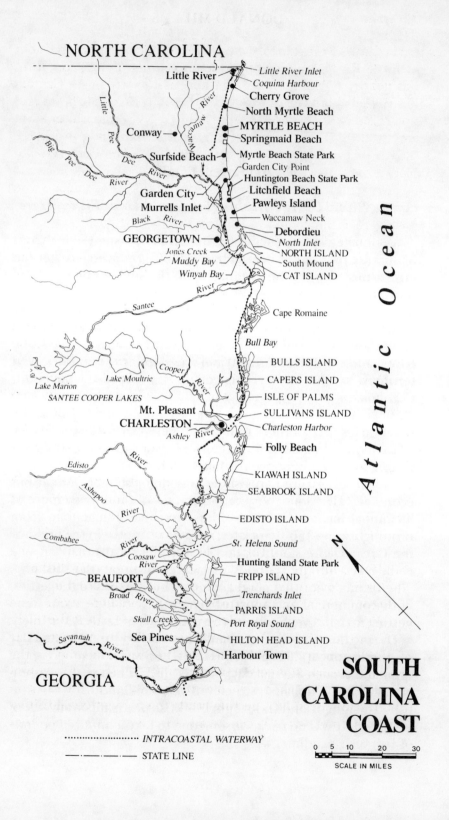

NORTH CAROLINA

Little River
Little River Inlet
Coquina Harbour
Cherry Grove
North Myrtle Beach
MYRTLE BEACH
Conway
Springmaid Beach
Surfside Beach
Myrtle Beach State Park
Garden City Point
Huntington Beach State Park
Garden City
Litchfield Beach
Murrells Inlet
Pawleys Island
Waccamaw Neck
Debordieu
GEORGETOWN
North Inlet
Jones Creek
NORTH ISLAND
Muddy Bay
South Mound
Winyah Bay
CAT ISLAND

Little Pee Dee
Big Pee Dee River
Dee River
Waccamaw River
Black River
Santee River

Cape Romaine

Santee

Bull Bay

Cooper River
BULLS ISLAND
Lake Moultrie
CAPERS ISLAND
Lake Marion
ISLE OF PALMS
SANTEE COOPER LAKES
Mt. Pleasant
SULLIVANS ISLAND
CHARLESTON
Charleston Harbor
Ashley River
Folly Beach

Edisto River
KIAWAH ISLAND
Ashepoo River
SEABROOK ISLAND

EDISTO ISLAND

Combahee River
St. Helena Sound
Coosaw River
Hunting Island State Park
BEAUFORT
FRIPP ISLAND
Broad River
Trenchards Inlet
Skull Creek
PARRIS ISLAND
Savannah River
Port Royal Sound
Sea Pines
HILTON HEAD ISLAND
Harbour Town

GEORGIA

Atlantic Ocean

N

SOUTH
CAROLINA
COAST

············ INTRACOASTAL WATERWAY
———— STATE LINE

0 5 10   20   30

SCALE IN MILES

Handlines were standard equipment on that first headboat out of Little River, captained by Lawrence Long. Long's son, Billy, was nearby working on his own boat as I chatted with Captain Frank Juel about the way it used to be. Billy asked me how I had done fishing at the jetty. I reported that I saw one winter trout taken that day, but a pair of anglers bottomfishing inside the mouth of the inlet told me that they had taken both red and black drum the week before. Apparently, the phase of the moon was wrong for this day. Still, the chance to talk to someone who had fished Little River all his life more than made up for my pleasant but unproductive fishing.

I first met Captain Juel in 1974 when he took a dozen anglers from Francis Marion College and U.S.C.-Coastal Carolina out for a day of snapper bank fishing on one of his many boats named the "Hurricane." Eight different "Hurricanes" have been skippered by him, beginning with an Air-Sea Rescue boat that he had bought in Miami at a government auction after the war. "After the war I began running trips on my first boat and we still fished with handlines." Captain Juel's first snapper bank trips were run in 1948 and overnight trips were especially popular.

"It took us four hours to get out there. We would start fishing after midnight and by dawn we would have the box filled with three thousand pounds of grouper and snapper. Our only navigational aid was the compass." Like Morehead City's Captain Sonny Davis, he shipped boxes of grouper and red snapper to the New York market and got in return only a bill for freight. Today such boxes of fish would be worth very good money as gourmet magazines and increased travel have expanded the public's concept of fine seafood to encompass not only lobster and shrimp but the dwellers on our offshore reefs.

As Juel talked he reflected on offshore fishing over the years. "It slowed down when those Russian trawlers showed up. Two 200-foot trawlers and a big mother boat would come out there and the trawlers would sweep the reef from one end to the other. We had to get out of the way. Since they stopped that, the grouper has come back up." He noted that commercial boats from Florida come up to work the reefs in the summer—his son still longlines for grouper and snapper in 600 feet of water in the fall and winter. (He was, in fact, getting ready to go commercial fishing himself the next day.) When asked about traps, he pointed out that seabass will move back on a reef right after it's been trapped. "I don't believe trapping hurts fishing, but we do need a minimum size on bass, snapper, and grouper, whether they're caught on hook or line or by nets. . . . I don't believe a saltwater license would help."

My memories of Captain Juel are many. He was the first person to tell me the fisherman's name for the strawberry grouper, "Kitty Mitchell." (Years later Dr. Gene Huntsman from Beaufort, North Carolina, would trace the name's etymology to the fishermen-patrons of a "sporting house" on Florida's Gulf Coast run by a madam named Kitty Mitchell who had dark red hair and whose hospitality was recalled by fishermen hauling in strawberry colored grouper from the Gulf bottom.)

I also observed Captain Juel having to deal, patiently but firmly, with a drunk passenger who insisted on climbing up to the wheel house at nine in the morning to confer with the skipper. "All I need is for him to fall down and break a leg or worse—I don't know why I'm in this business," was his comment at the time. That evening as the captain navigated the inlet he did so very gingerly, for the tide was just beginning to come in and the jetties were still four years away. When the bow touched bottom the "Hurricane" was making no more than two knots and it was easy to back off and wait. But it was evidence of why an all-weather, all-tide inlet was needed by fishermen.

The last time I fished with Captain Juel was in the early '80s on board young Captain Steve Speros's first brand-new "Hurricane." Captain Juel was helping out, and both the young captain and the old captain were having a chuckle as a temporary deckhand, two weeks out of the U.S. Navy, was poring over navigational charts to help the two skippers get to their offshore destination. Neither had the heart to tell the young man they didn't need help navigating the boat. What was needed was getting the squid cut, the bait passed out, and the fish taken off their customers' lines and into the on-deck cooler.

Little River Notes: Flounder fishing can be outstanding at nearby Cherry Grove. Stripers are taken in the Intracoastal Waterway from September through March, but don't bother fishing until at least three or four days after a heavy rain. Excellent winter trout fishing may be had at Coquina Harbour, but some anglers have complained bitterly about heavy pressure from netters hurting the fishing there in recent years. Spot, croaker, flounder, and crabs may be harvested throughout the area. (Even if you don't fish, catch the "Blue Crab Arts and Crafts Festival" held annually in May.)

There is much sheltered water that is easily accessible to small and large boats. The mouth of the inlet can have huge swells, even when the ocean is fairly calm. Caution is needed by small boat anglers. Fortunately, the clean beaches are reached only by boat, but care should be taken wading or swimming. Winter trout are caught from the rocks, but fishing from a jetty is not my cup of tea: too many ways to break a bone or lose a fish. A writer in a state government publication once suggested that one has to be agile to jump from rock to rock, or words to that effect. "You have to be nuts to jump from rock to rock on a slippery jetty," is the way a local angler responded. Be careful at any inlet on our coast, whether you're in a boat on the water or fishing from the rocks.

North Myrtle Beach: The King Arthur Mackerel Circus

"There were giants in those days," it says in the Old Testament. The Colossus of Rhodes was one of the seven wonders of the world. "I remember the days when it was no trick to fill the box with kings by noon," said the old-timer sitting outside the North Myrtle Beach marina. The ideas are not unrelated. The giant is Arthur Smith, the monument is the jetties at Little River, and if the boxes aren't being filled with king mackerel anymore, fishermen are still spending millions of dollars to fish in the Arthur Smith—one of his friends calls it the "King Arthur"— King Mackerel Tournament and its many spinoffs from Florida to New York to California.

I must confess that I have fished the tournament only once, and that under protest. It's not that Arthur Smith isn't a friendly guy, and it's not that his luck with the weather is mostly rotten, but rather that I usually am scheduled to teach a class just about the time that a flotilla of 500 boats is hitting the swells at the mouth of Little River Inlet. When my eight o'clock class at Coastal Carolina College asks me why I'm not out fishing, I just turn on the weather radio and let them hear about the northeast winds and eight-foot waves. Of course, it's not always that bad. Sometimes it's worse.

A case in point is the one year I was able to fish the tournament thanks to a class schedule that left me free on Tuesday and Thursday that semester and a weather system that scrubbed the first day of the tournament and turned Saturday into a half-day of king mackerel fishing. A quartet of determined anglers from Virginia had inveigled my name from a friend of mine on the Eastern Shore. I was to be their local guide, fishing the Arthur Smith Tournament with them. I explained that I was better with trout than with kings, and that I had Friday classes, but I could run out with them Thursday and get them started live-bait fishing. "We're strictly trolling specialists," was the reply. White marlin off Virginia Beach and all that, right? Wrong for the Arthur Smith Tournament, usually won by live baits, slow trolled, drifted, or float fished. But the Virginians were persistent, so I went. I still have the scars.

We put the boat in at the old ramp adjacent to what was then Ron Tom Marina and across the Intracoastal Waterway from tournament headquarters at Palmetto Shores Marina. Some boat company's fishing team was ruining the manufacturer's reputation and making life miserable for the poor sailors launching their boats at our ramp by roaring back and forth down the Waterway in their logoed fishing machine, throwing up five foot swells that made launching a challenge. But we got in.

We spent the next few hours jockeying for position and safety with hundreds of other boats waiting for the go-ahead signal for the day, but it never came. Seems that the mouth of the inlet looked too dangerous as outgoing tide and incoming winds met. By late morning the tournament fishing had been scratched for the day, but a half hour later we decided that we could fish, and after a bit of roughness in the mouth, we headed offshore on what was becoming a pretty day. The seas were calming, the sun was shining, and 30 miles out we found the kings ready to hit. Nothing over 15 pounds went into the box, but it was at least a shake-down for the next day.

The crew of the "Gin-Jen" fished without me on Friday, for I had to be back in class; their luck and Arthur Smith's was the better for it. They had a full day of tournament fishing despite rough seas. Unfortunately, the trolled spoons and rigged baits didn't put anything more than a few "snakes" (small kings) in the box. When I got the news I was relieved: If I were a jinx it was only with regard to the weather. The tournament was more than half over, but Saturday, usually reserved for the awards ceremony and king mackerel fish fry, would be a half fishing day to give all the boats one more chance at the big one.

The north winds did blow. It was a fresh, bright gorgeous day, the kind of day the Roman poet described when he contrasted the people standing on a promontory in the warm sunshine and fresh air looking down on a frothy sea and mariners struggling with their tiny sailing vessels, the kind of day Stephen Crane described in his classic short story, "The Open Boat," with the glorious—as long as you weren't in the boat—interplay of water, wind, and reflected sunshine. The further offshore we got, the rougher it became. Glittering on shore was the Hilton Hotel and the high-rise condominiums that had already begun to change the North Myrtle Beach skyline. Down in the cockpit of the "Gin-Jen," swathed in foul weather gear, I was trying to get our lines out to troll for that one big king that would make the trip worthwhile.

We turned the boat back toward the north to troll toward shore and the first of many waves came smashing over the bow, over the cabin, and into the cockpit. But that is the story of tournament fishing: once you've wagered on yourself with your entry fee you have to take pot luck on the weather. Well, at least the sun was shining, the beer was cold, and the sandwiches tasted just fine after our early morning rising, even though we had to brace ourselves in the cabin to eat and drink.

"Fish-on!" the skipper yelled, and I grabbed for the bending rod. Every hit in a tournament with cash prizes is potentially your entry fee or better—first prize that year was some $15,000 or so in cash plus a boat, motor, and trailer, I believe—and a certain edge was thus added to our basic competitive, tournament fever. "Perhaps money isn't everything, but it will make me forget some of the struggles of these past few days."

It is disappointing when the fish gives in easily, another eight pounder at best, but it is still a fish, a challenge tricked, potential succulent king steaks for the table. I brace myself against the gunwale, forget the soaking coming over the boat from the waves, and I reel. Someone opens the fish box that is not at the stern but toward the cabin, and I back up a little more, too far in fact. As the fish is swung over the the side I take a step backward, trip, and land on my fanny in the ice box. The next week Dr. Wilson, my family physician, told me I needed surgery for a hernia. I still suspect that the rough-weather king helped make a surgeon neighbor of mine, good Dr. Hal Holmes, a few bucks richer.

One of the delights in pulling up the lines after a three-small-fish day is that you are under no pressure to get back in port by any deadline the way one of the boats farther offshore than us was. We heard him over the radio pleading for an extension, and we saw him bouncing by, trying to drive his boat impossibly fast in incredibly rough seas. We lifted our beers in a toast and prayed that his boat would not disintegrate on the next bounce as we slowly made our way through the glorious waves and white water to the tranquility of the inlet.

Perhaps the best part of any Arthur Smith Tournament is the awards presentation. Country musicians dominate, naturally. The colorful freebie caps of the participating teams give the crowd a festive air. One year at Vereen's Marina there was even one of those carnival games of chance at which a young man from Clemson was dropping fives and tens in an attempt to win his girl friend a big stuffed animal. The various flags and banners of beer, boat, and chewing tobacco sponsors add to the color of the occasion. And everybody attends, even those beautiful women who decorated the decks of the big yachts that (wisely) never left the dock. The reason is that someone's name will be pulled from the barrel and announced as a winner of $10,000 in cash. Attendance is always good, at least until the drawing.

So we drank our cold beer and enjoyed our king mackerel steaks—the public, by the way, is invited to buy a ticket for lunch, but only the participants in the tournament draw for the prizes—and applauded the winning teams. They not only braved the weather, but they caught big kings, and that's the bottom line—along with the fun. One final statistic, from *Field & Stream* magazine: " ... during the two-day 1980 Arthur Smith King Mackerel Tournament in South Carolina, 1,844 anglers spent $650,000 to catch 3,500 pounds of fish. That makes each of those kingfish worth $185.71 per pound."

The awards ceremony and king mackerel cookout of the Arthur Smith King Mackerel Tournament is always well attended.

And that doesn't include the cost of a hernia repair. I should add that Arthur Smith got tired of his bad luck with the weather in October and moved his king mackerel tournament to late September in 1985. Of course, his weather luck didn't change. The first day of the Ninth Annual Arthur Smith King Mackerel Tournament was also the day that Hurricane Gloria had zeroed in on the Carolina coast. So don't ask me why I don't fish the King Arthur Tournament. But there are thousands of fishermen who wouldn't miss it for the world. And even without a statue, the jetties at Little River are a lasting monument to a country musician who liked to fish for kings out in the ocean off North Myrtle Beach.

Myrtle Beach: "You Can't Catch Fish on Credit"

People who are very good at what they do, enjoy doing it, and still don't take it all too seriously, are very easy to be with. The ability to chuckle at one's own foibles and at the common failings of mankind may not be very strong among upwardly mobile professionals, but from Erasmus and St. Thomas More to R.D.

Brigham and family it is a side of the human spirit that makes such people good companions. Brigham never wrote a book, but his fishing exploits are certainly worthy of one.

Stop in at City Bait and Tackle in Myrtle Beach sometime and savor the atmosphere. One or more of the Brighams will be presiding over sales of bait, tackle, and beer. The other members of the family will probably be out hunting or fishing, more likely the latter. As patriarch of the clan, R.D., replete with grin, moustache, sparkling eyes, and a cup to catch an occasional stream of tobacco juice, will be observing and commenting. He views even his own fishing ironically, "You can't catch fish on credit" being his standard comment on a cleaned hook, whether he's fishing for bream or crappies in the Rice Fields, for flounder in the creeks, or for snapper offshore. R.D. is already immortalized by a flounder hole in Murrells Inlet that used to produce large numbers of large flatfish. When all else fails, I drop a live shrimp or mud minnow in the "Brigham Hole" to rescue dinner from a slow day. In April and November, as well as the months in between, it still produces flatfish for sons Roy, Dean, and George as they troll slowly, waiting for that solitary tap that indicates the mud minnow is in the process of being swallowed by a fat flatfish. Tina Brigham, R.D.'s wife and the most determined angler of the family—never kid her about not having as many fish as you, for she will stay fishing until you drop and probably be 20 pounds ahead when you quit—will fish the same area for spot and croaker, as R.D. patiently drifts a shrimp for winter trout.

R.D. is in good part responsible for the South Carolina record channel bass which was caught by a fishing companion of his, Archie Taylor of nearby Conway. They were out fishing in Murrells Inlet for flounder in February when Taylor hooked into what turned out to be a 75-pound fish. "I never stopped that motor for four hours," Brigham recalls. "We ran all over creation and finally managed to slide the fish up on a mudbank." Unfortunately the International Game Fish Association did not recognize the fish as a world record because, so some functionary explained, they were concerned that the other hook on the flounder rig Taylor was using could have snagged the fish and thus put it outside the pale of IGFA regulations. "Don, that other hook was not in the fish." Even if it was, Taylor still deserves a line in the IGFA record book. R.D. Brigham should get a footnote, too.

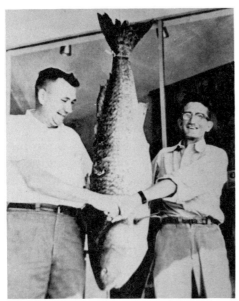

Archie Taylor, left, caught this 75-pound channel bass in February of 1965 while trolling for flounder with R.D. Brigham, right. Although the fish is 21 pounds heavier than the record fish for its line class (14-pound test), it was disqualified on a technicality.

Photo by John Devine

Son Roy, co-proprietor of the City Bait and Tackle emporium, is one of the best flounder fishermen who ever graced Second Avenue Pier, fishing with live mullet or mud minnows under the pier, or even launching his small boat in calm weather to fish around what is left of the end of the pier destroyed by Hurricane Hazel. In the fall he spends much of his time throwing a net from the pier for mullet and the rest of the day filleting and salting the mullet. Anglers on their way north to the Outer Banks or south to the barrier islands stop in for a supply of City Bait mullet; "it stays on the hook," perhaps the Myrtle Beach equivalent of "Powder Milk Biscuits . . . they sure are expeditious."

Wife Tina and daughter-in-law Jeanne specialize in surf fishing, which means sitting in a canvas chair in their bathing suits waiting for a whiting or pompano to hit their baits, usually mole crabs (sand fleas) that have had part of their shell carefully peeled back. If anyone catches pompano consistently in July and August it is Tina, and anyone attempting to buy bait at her tackle shop is informed in no uncertain terms that the best baits in life, sand fleas, are free for the taking at low tide all along our beaches. (This is being written before beach renourishment, of course; whether the $5 million worth of trucked sand stays where it's put or is washed away by the ocean, the question still remains whether the sand fleas and all the fish—and fishermen—to whom they are an important part of the beach will still be there after renourishment is history.)

The Brighams have never been much on summer trout (weakfish) and occasionally refer to the fish of less than a pound as "Springmaid trout," Springmaid Pier being the most productive pier in the area for these smaller cousins (at least in this area) of the spotted sea trout. They don't fish from Springmaid, or any other pier for that matter, for king mackerel, even when a half dozen or more kings a day are being taken from the pier. "We can always run out with Buck for kings," referring to charter boat skipper and friend Buck Kempson with whom they fish for fun.

When saltwater fishing slows down, the Brighams direct their attention to the rivers and the Intracoastal Waterway for bream, shellcracker, redfin trout, crappie, bass, and stripers. One of them was asked whether he fished around Cape Hatteras. "Never," was his response, "there's just too much fishing around here."

Murrells Inlet: A Collective Memory of Oystering, Crabbing, Fishing

The Indian tribes who harvested oysters from Murrells Inlet, the plantation owners from the Rice Fields who had their summer houses here, and the slaves who brought in crabs, mullet, and shrimp from the inlet would not recognize the place if they returned, at least not at first. The same might be said by anyone who remembers Murrells Inlet as it was 50 or even 25 years ago. But get away from the commercial districts, get away from the condominium construction, take a small boat into the back creeks or across the inlet toward Huntington Beach State Park, turn your back on the jetties and the expensive houses built precariously on sand, fashionable hostages to the first hurricane that hits Garden City Point straight on, and you will find that the inlet is still a nice place to be in any season of the year.

Even for a newcomer like myself who has fished Murrells Inlet

116

for just a dozen years, the inlet has memories that not even the juggernaut of commercialization can erase. After all, one can still harvest shrimp, blueclaw crabs, clams, and oysters here in the middle of the ninth decade of the twentieth century. There are still flounder to be caught in the creeks in early spring and at the rocks toward summer. Last Saturday (I am writing this just after Thanksgiving) the Shriners of Murrells Inlet held a fishing tournament to raise funds for the Crippled Children's Hospital in Greenville, South Carolina. The top fish was a speckled trout going close to eight pounds, and two almost-six-pounders vied for second. And there are still people there who will fight to keep the inlet a nice place to shrimp, clam, and fish.

Murrells Inlet is where I spend most of my fishing time, for the boat ramp at Inlet Port Marina is just a half hour from my driveway. My memories are many:

Captain Tommy Sing standing on the bridge of his "Flying

U.S. Secretary of Education Dr. T.E. Bell wanted "to get away from it all for just a few hours" while visiting South Carolina to give a speech at a convention of educators. Red drum and bluefish from next to the Murrells Inlet jetties cooperated for the visiting angler.

Fisher" and hooking five king mackerel—they would weigh over 90 pounds—on live baits while a boatload of college anglers from the United States and Canada were catching enough seabass to feed the youngsters at the Horry County Shelter Home for a winter of fish dinners. Or the same captain telling me I wasn't holding my mouth right as he hooked eight winter trout in a row to my none on an October morning fishing from his little Boston Whaler. (His advice took, for I hooked the next six in a row.)

Buck Kempson puts his "Mermaid II" over a ledge some 40 miles out of the inlet and in two drifts I take my first two genuine red snapper after four years of watching anglers such as Skip Opalko hang the "genuines." Buck will later that day hang the "Mermaid II" on a sandbar inside the mouth of the inlet, this in the days before dredging and the jetties. A young man, first mate on a headboat, remarks on the paucity of black seabass on a summer half-day trip. "It's our own fault," he admits. "Last winter we trapped the hell out of the inshore reefs for blackfish and there are very few left for our summer customers."

There is sadness among the memories: the first spottail bass expedition one April finds us trolling along the rocks past what is left of the wreckage of the sportfishing boat "The Natural Lady." A stormy day, darkness, and the submerged rocks of the north jetty had cost the lives of three young people on the day after the jetties were officially dedicated. The 11-year-old niece of a friend of mine asks about the debris. When told the story, she remarks that "they ought to get that wreckage off the rocks." The ocean eventually sweeps them clean. The memory never disappears entirely.

There are more images: Men and women, old and young, harvest oysters and clams in the winter light. For five dollars I get a sack of clams for roasting with a dozen extra-large clams for chowder thrown in. But that was years ago. In the summer, it is families dragging a seine net for shrimp and sometimes filling half a cooler. Little old ladies in tennis shoes run their own five-horse motorboat to a likely creek. A girl who works at one of the marinas catches a mess of three-quarter-pound grouper—yes grouper, for the inlet is a nursery for offshore waters—from the dock!

Debbie Dodson, now Mrs. James Dickey, fights a 40-pound bull dolphin leaping behind the boat in one of the early Gulf

Stream Marina billfishing tournaments. Young Jack Orr catches his first winter trout with me on a cold December day and two years later takes second place in the Arthur Smith King Mackerel Tournament with a 35-pound king. J.B. Orr, his dad, sends us to a hotspot for flounder, and Charley Johnson takes not only some nice flounder but a big blue that turns into a king mackerel bait.

Our guests are memorable, too. *New York Times* outdoor writer Nelson Bryant trolls up big spottail bass on mud minnows on consecutive rainy, cold March days at the jetties. Nobody else had tried fishing for them and we take the fish for a two-hour stretch mid-way in the incoming tide. The fish quit early. On another trip my younger son, Donnie, and I are asked to host Dr. T.E. Bell, President Reagan's first secretary of education. We have to wait for the tide to drop before we fill half a cooler with summer fish: blues, seabass, and, again, spottail bass. Our visitor is pleasantly surprised at both the fishing and the well-preserved marshland at the heart of the inlet. On another trip we watch a writer friend, George Reiger, first hook a big channel bass that breaks his freshwater graphite rod and then a five-pound flounder that he carefully guides into our outstretched net. His thoughtful and engaging book *Wanderer on My Native Shore*, nominated for a Pulitzer Prize, devotes a section to the fish and birds of Murrells Inlet. "I hope this place doesn't wind up looking like the Jersey Shore," he comments as I point out new and planned construction sites. I share his hope, but more than hopes are needed.

Man's collective memories are more reliable than those of any individual. For more about Murrells Inlet, talk to those we have mentioned, or Captains Hoss Johnson, Bill Moeller, Tommy Swatzel, and Everett Ayers or Frank Seiveno at Captain Dick's Marina or Captains Charley Gibbs, Don Lash, and Mike Brewster or Barry Schoch at Inlet Port Marina or the older members of the Nance family or Wallace Lee at their seafood restaurants or Clark Willcox at the Hermitage or Dr. Charles Joyner at U.S.C.-Coastal Carolina College or fishermen like Johnny McDowell and Lem Winesett as they troll their grubs or cast their plugs on a late fall evening in Murrells Inlet. Better still, launch your jon boat or cruiser at the ramp shaded by ancient live oaks next to Belin Methodist Church on U.S. Business Highway 17. Go see for yourself that Murrells Inlet is worth saving.

Waccamaw Neck: From Pawleys Inlet to North Island

"Ma'am, I own the land to the right of us and the land to the left of us." The speaker was Mister Buck, the early nineteenth-century founder of Bucksport, a settlement well inland from the ocean, up the Waccamaw River toward Conway. The punch line of the story is "Them's mighty fine bream." The rest of the story is available from old-timers in the Waccamaw Neck section of South Carolina, but I deliberately omit it in the hope that the reader's curiosity about the history of this whole changing region of coastal Carolina will be stimulated.

Bounded by the ocean on one side and the Waccamaw River on the other, with Winyah Bay and North Island to the south, the Waccamaw Neck section of historic Georgetown County includes Murrells Inlet, Litchfield Beach, Pawleys Island, Debordieu, and North Island. As the last remnants of some of the nineteenth-century rice plantations are sold to developers of "lifestyles," it is worth reflecting on the lifestyles once supported by this part of our coast.

"Doc" Lachicotte is a living example of the changes in lifestyles that have occurred in this region. Ten years ago it was nothing for him to take a dozen saltwater trout in an hour or two of late afternoon fishing . . . the morning may have been spent hunting . . . but when I last met him, it was at Wachesaw Plantation, a new private golf club. Lachicotte was talking about taking golf lessons, because the fish just aren't around anymore. Ten years ago he would have chuckled at the idea of preferring golf to fishing: things have changed.

Things have changed at Pawleys Island—not enough parking spaces for visitors in the summer. But the inlet between Pawleys and Litchfield Beach is still a good place to fish for trout or spot, particularly in late November and December. Just before Christmas on a warm but rainy and blustery day I needed help carrying two stringers of trout and spottail bass from the beach—this was in the mid '70s—but the other day the word was out that the trout were back. Spot, too, may still be taken from the beach, and at the south end of Pawleys Island the incoming tide in late spring and summer is always good for some small bluefish with an occasional Spanish mackerel as a surprise.

Things have not changed as much at Debordieu, also written as "DuBordieu," "DeBordieu," and "Debidue," but pronounced "Debby Do." The real treat for the fisherman or nature lover is an invitation from someone who has access to this very private section or to the Baruch estate, now given to Clemson University and the University of South Carolina for marine and forestry research, to fish North Inlet for trout or spottail. Billy Foxworth, his son "Doc," and I have harvested and eaten raw the succulent oysters of Jones Creek, our access being not through the gate but the long way around across Muddy Bay from Georgetown. Come to think of it, we ran out of gas a mile short of our destination and needed a tow to Belle Isle Marina on Winyah Bay.

My luck has been worse. On an April trip for oysters at North Inlet the winds kept me and Mitch Godwin from getting across Muddy Bay. We spend the night as uninvited guests of Mr. Yawkey's estate, North Island segment. The stars were out, the temperature in the 60's, and there were no mosquitoes. I steamed clams, while broiling carefully cleaned and skinned catfish and eels over an open fire that Mitch had built. Our firebuilder lost his appetite for some reason when I announced the dinner menu—perhaps his Cherokee ancestors would not have been so finicky—but we were in good spirits as we crawled under our foul weather gear next to a roaring fire for a good night's sleep. Unfortunately, the gnats were not informed that their presence was not required. The next morning I saw from Mitch's swollen lips and heard from my mumbled speech the results of getting too close to nature without benefit of the right repellent.

As long as the waters stay clean, the Waccamaw River and the inlets of the Waccamaw Neck and Winyah Bay will be good places to fish. One estimate of "only 20 million gallons a day of treated effluent" going into the Waccamaw River near Murrells Inlet has made a lot of river bass fishermen, as well as saltwater anglers, very nervous, however. The story of Waccamaw Neck is still being written.

Georgetown: Winyah Bay, Land of Adventure

There is some good fishing in Winyah Bay, south of Georgetown, South Carolina, but I would be less than candid if I did not note that for the unwary or unlucky it can be a dangerous place to fish. Fortunately, that is not usually the case. On a calm and sunny February morning when the stripers are biting just before low slack water, on a late spring day when the flounder are putting a serious bend into your cane pole as you dip minnows around the edge of a favorite rockpile, in the August sun as you concentrate on the sensitive bite of a hungry sheepshead trying to steal your fiddler crab bait, on a soft fall afternoon when the spottail or spotted sea trout are hitting cut mullet in the surf at South Island, the bay and its nearby waters can seem to be a paradise for anglers, the gift of a beneficent Providence.

Or survey Winyah Bay, a beer in your hand and the big cooler of your sportfishing boat filled with yellowfin tuna, dolphin, and kings from the Gulf Stream. Recall the fight and imagine the taste of those succulent fish steaks, as you head in past the South Mound, that pile of rocks that marks one side of the approach to the mouth of the bay, itself a fine fishing spot for sheepshead and drum in season. Summer trout, black drum, sturgeon for netters, at least in the not so long ago good old days, all are part of the pleasant picture the bay presents to those who are there at the right time. Add shrimp, clams, oysters, and the knowledge that thousands of people love Winyah Bay enough to have been terrified by the thought of a refinery being built there a few years back. Fortunately, according to some, both the oil crisis and the threat of a refinery disappeared. But the dangers of Winyah Bay remain for those who are unlucky or careless.

What are the dangers of the bay? First of all, it is long, wide at points, and shallow. A northeast wind pushing against an outgoing tide can raise some very big waves, while strong winds from the west or southwest can also kick things up, even in shallow Muddy Bay, where Mitch Godwin and I almost swamped his flat-bottomed boat as we came out of a creek gloating over the bushels of oysters we had harvested one April afternoon. In colder weather an overturned boat can put one's life at risk on Winyah Bay or even on its islands or in its creeks.

Near the entrance to Winyah Bay at the South Mound, amidst treacherous currents, with darkness long descended and the rain blowing down in sheets driven by a cold northeast wind, I once watched Captain Wayne Strickland secure the troubled and hapless and then helpless "Flying Fisher II" after its towline from

Strickland's "Carolina Princess" had snapped. The old fishing boat had become disabled some 40 miles out in a stormy Atlantic. After eight hours of torturously slow towing in unrelenting nine-foot seas, the towline had snapped in the worst of places, just off the rocks at the mouth of the bay. Only a cool head and able seamanship saved boat and passengers from sea and rocks. The skill and bravery of the young captain are worth remembering, but I hope that I will never again have to depend so desperately on another mortal.

In the cold of winter, fishermen and hunters have found themselves fighting to stay alive, their boats disabled and drifting in the cold currents of the lower bay. Some have not survived. One January day when the water temperature was in the low 40's at best and the air temperature in the low 20's, I was racing my aluminum boat at full speed down the bay to try for stripers. It suddenly dawned on me that if I ever turned over I could survive for little more than an hour before succumbing to hypothermia, the killing effect of cold on the body of an angler clinging to his overturned boat. Many a summer sailor, caught in the wind and waves of the bay, has wished that his trip south of Georgetown had been less of an an adventure.

True, there are big fish here, but not even if the too-quickly exploited and overfished sturgeon population is protected for years to come will it return to its seemingly inexhaustible abundance of the late '70s. Ask R.Y. Cathou about it if you are lucky enough to catch him at his fish house on the waterfront. Rene Yve's father came to New England from France in the late nineteenth century and eventually made his way down to Georgetown where his knowledge of fishing "bateaux" and his willingness to work hard got him into a partnership in a commercial fishing dock. His son has been in the same business for over half a century, but has not run his own shrimp boat in almost 10 years.

"It's a young man's work," R.Y. Cathou says even as he clambers about the slippery ways of his "dry" dock. "Clamming, now that's hard work," he adds as he guides a "bateau" to a new berth and ties its line. Pay little mind to his oaths, for the man is worried about making a living for himself and all those he employs with a bay that is experiencing the everyday pressures of the twentieth century: pollution, population, and development. Ask him about the lady "who has blood that's bluer than yours or mine" to whom he shipped his fourteen-dollar-a-jar caviar in the '70s—before inflation. Things have gotten worse since then, but Cathou, troubled with arthritis, toughs it out in the eighth decade of his life in Georgetown. Tough as the bay he is, but a lot more understanding, his colorful adjectives redolent of how tough it is to wrest a living from this beautiful but contemptuous bay.

If you stop at Georgetown Landing Marina, talk to Captain Owen Daly about how charter boat fishing used to be, when he could drag a couple of spoons behind the boat and fill the box with king mackerel by 11 in the morning and now you're a hero if on a beautiful summer day you take a dozen. Ask him about kings leaping as high as his eye level on the flying bridge of his charterboat, the "Mar-Har IV," or go out with him and let him hook you up with a sky-climbing billfish or a yellowfin tuna that is off to the races. But all the while, notice how he keeps a weather eye out and listens to N.O.A.A. (National Oceanic and Atmospheric Administration, but say "Noah") radio. If you go down to the sea out of Winyah Bay or even fish within its spacious confines, so should you.

R.Y. Cathou surveys the world from the entrance to his wholesale fish business on the waterfront in Georgetown, a business he inherited from his father who came to South Carolina from France via New England.

Charleston: "You Got to Pay Your Dues"

Early in the spring of 1960 a captain of a 47-foot headboat was on his way back to North Carolina. He and his crew decided to do some bottom fishing off Charleston as they made their way up the coast. They started in 140 feet of water and worked out to 200 feet, fishing for "genuines" (red snapper). "We were throwing away scamp grouper anywhere from 20 to 25 pounds apiece. We were getting 50 cents a pound for them, but we couldn't get rid of the groupers. . . . I couldn't get a nickel a pound for groupers. So we bring up doubleheaders of them big flatbellies weighing roughly 50 to 75 pounds and turn 'em loose and let 'em go." That's how it was in the Gulf Stream off Charleston just a quarter of a century ago.

Over half a century ago, Charleston's fishermen became famous, thanks to George Gershwin and *Porgy and Bess*, for fishing the "blackfish banks." The waters 10 to 30 miles off the coast still produce good catches of black seabass, the "blackfish" Porgy's friends sang about, but neither in the numbers nor size of yesterday.

Even in the 1950s, the fisherman who went out in his small boat on the Wando River to fish for saltwater trout or striped bass on an overcast winter day would find that he had the fish to himself. Now, according to one old-timer, even in the nastiest weather, he has a lot of company. "You can still get a mess of trout but they are not here the way they used to be. Because of the fishing pressure, everybody's cut of the pie has become smaller."

Things have also changed for the sport and commercial fishermen of Charleston, but there is still good fishing to be had and a future for the sport hereabouts, at least according to one courageous angler. I say "courageous" not just because he has spent some two decades fishing the waters of Charleston Harbor after a railroading accident cost him his right arm and right leg. But "Creekman," Waring W. Hills, has spoken up continually for the wise and even gentlemanly use of our marine resources. Whether he is sitting in his wheelchair beside a pond at nearby Kiawah Island showing youngsters how to flip a cane pole and floatline for bream and bass, or testifying at a public hearing to control netting of gamefish or seek reasonable size and creel limits on marine species, his cheerful, thoughtful, and sometimes gruff voice has spoken loudly for the future of coastal fishing. He shakes his head sadly as he notes that there's "absolutely no respect anymore," respect for the environment, respect for the future of the sport, respect even for other fishermen who may have found where the first channel bass of the spring or the last winter trout of the fall were biting.

Despite the increased pressure on the fish, Creekman insists that there's still a lot of good fishing around Charleston. Creekman likes to be one of the first fishermen out at the end of the jetties in early spring, especially when a few balmy days succeed the northeast winds of March. He gives good advice: "Fish cut mullet on bottom at the jetties or cast a Mirrolure over the edge of the rocks. The spottails (channel bass) will go from three pounds on up to some you can't stop." There are also bluefish here in the spring, he notes, and some surprises, too: Last year he took some friends out to help shake down their new sportfishing boat and suggested they cast popping plugs for bluefish around the jetties. "Well, it wasn't a blue, but a 13-pound king and I had to run the fish down because all they had on their reels was eight-pound test line." There are always surprises at the jetties.

"I like the incoming tide because the water is cleaner—falling water is muddy, but rising water turns beautiful and you can bust 'em sometimes. There are sheepshead there year-round and you can never tell what's going to hit."

In the summer, Creekman likes to fish for flounder with mud minnows for bait around the rocks at Sullivan's Island. He notes that some patient anglers used to bring their tackle to the Battery, cast out their lines for flounder, and settle back in canvas chairs to wait for a bite. "Out off the island we sometimes fish for them with live shrimp or mud minnows on a float rig and (he says this in a conspiratorial tone) the mud minnow also makes a great bait for channel bass and winter trout (spotted sea trout)." But if you want real action in the harbor, Creekman suggests, try for jack crevalle.

"I've seen jacks five feet long and I once chased one for two miles trying to keep it from running all our line. Thirty pounders

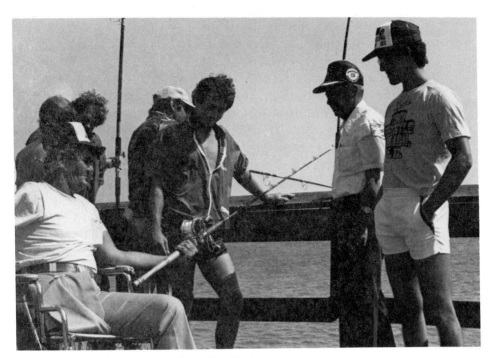

W.W. Hills, better known as "Creekman," talks about tackle and fishing during a seminar program on fishing held on a coastal pier.

are not unusual in the harbor, but the trick is not hooking them but keeping them on the hook. If they get back into the school their hard and boney tails will cut your line. Fish tip-top high water and look for the fish to break out on the surface near points where currents converge." He sometimes uses Creek Chub lures—six- to eight-inch swimming plugs—cast on spinning tackle, but notes that a live shrimp, or even a dead one hooked through the side where it folds and popped over the surface, will almost always get a strike.

Creekman points out that one of the reasons that fishing for jack crevalle is still good is that the fish has no commercial value. "It's just fun to catch 'em and release 'em. The only way they are good to eat is if they're smoked."

One fish that definitely is good to eat is the striped bass, a fish that Creekman used to take in good numbers from the rivers flowing into Charleston Harbor. "I've fished all the way up the Ashley and up the Cooper to the tailrace canal and taken striped bass—the nastier the weather the better." He is sure that some stripers are still there, best in December after the weather turns cold and rotten.

Another "good eating" fish that can cause a lot of excitement is the king mackerel. "They're out there just where the color line changes, outside the harbor, from March until November," he points out, emphasizing that summer angling doesn't necessarily mean having to run far offshore. For years he directed one of the finest fishing tournaments ever devised by man, the Charleston Harbor Fishing Tournament, sponsored by the South Carolina State Ports Authority. Each month the largest fish of over a score of species would win a lottery ticket good for a drawing at the end of the year for boats, motors, trailers, and tackle. On occasion, the biggest flounder of a slow month might weigh just a pound but would be worth the same certificate given for a big blue marlin someone invested thousands of dollars in catching. But what's harder to catch, reasoned Creekman, a flounder when none are running or a big dolphin 70 miles out caught from a fishing machine costing six figures? It was a great idea, from a fisherman who believed in giving *everyone* a sporting chance, particularly the little guy.

When Creekman was the featured speaker at our intercollegiate fishing match and seminar, he emphasized not only the techniques of the fisherman but his need to put in his time on the water, trying each likely spot, each shellbank, each drop, experimenting with tides: "You got to pay your dues" was the way he summed it up. But he also expects that we pay our dues to protect what's left of coastal fishing. He wants to see a saltwater license with funds going not to the state's general fund but directly into research on fisheries or improvements for fishing such as landings and artificial reefs. Another benefit would be that federal funds allocated on the basis of number of licensed fishermen in the state would come into the Carolinas rather than go off to Texas and California, two states that license saltwater sportfishing. Finally, creel limits on saltwater trout and both minimum and maximum sizes on channel bass, in addition to limits, will help with these two gamefish, according to Creekman. These and, as he puts it, "a good hurricane to scour things out" on our overbuilt coastal islands would no doubt add another quarter of a century to the fishing career of a fisherman who refused to give up, even when he had to maneuver himself with one arm and one leg from wheelchair to jon boat.

Kiawah Island: Leaping Mullet and a Salt Pond Day

The nicest afternoon of fishing I have had on a barrier island occurred at a Kiawah Island salt pond. Now if I were a rich man—you may hum along, dear reader, in the manner of Zero Mostel, "deedle deedle deedle dum"—my wife would probably be after me to buy a house at Kiawah Island. It would not take much persuading, for Kiawah is as carefully planned and developed as any island on the Southeast coast, probably better than most. The dunes have been protected, the too-close-to-the-shore building that has had disastrous results at other island developments has been avoided, and such unglamorous creatures as the loggerhead turtle have found serene places for lying in, their beaches protected at night by a surrounding golf course, whose daytime inhabitants would never dream of messing with a nesting mother turtle. But the salt pond's the thing at Kiawah.

I had gone out with a "safari" for a cook's tour of the beach, but it took only one cast into the surf, muddy brown thanks to a brisk northeast wind, to convince my guide that surf fishing was not the order of the day. "Let's try a salt pond," he suggested. The pond in question had an inlet pipe that allowed the tide to rush water in, along with food in the form of small fishes, but once in the pond and growing, trout, spot, pinfish, spottail bass and flounder stayed put. And grew.

What was amazing was the size of the fish. One-pound pinfish, four-pound flounder, a number of fat spotted sea trout, and an abundance of shrimp and mullet were taken from the bank as the tide rushed on in, gushing out of the intake pipe four feet in the air and creating a current around the edges of which all the bigger fish in the pond seemed to gather like hungry guests at a luscious buffet.

Youngsters, oldsters, everyone who had a line in the water, whether baited with fresh shrimp, live mullet, or cut bait, was catching fish. I set a rod in a holder for my daughter to watch and a minute later the rod was throbbing and line was going out against the drag. Far out on the pond, a red drum splashed to the surface, even among the large fish of this feeding and even at a distance, the biggest fish of the day. Sara gamely pumped

The author's daughter, Sara, battled this red drum on light tackle in a salt pond on Kiawah Island. Dad tagged and released the fish, which eluded anglers for a year before it was caught again.

Photo by Patricia Millus

away and the fish grudgingly came toward the bank. I tried to encourage her, but the thought of the light hook we were using bending or pulling out of the jaw of that spottail put an edge on my feelings.

I called for help from the other anglers in the form of a landing net. Someone handed me a crab net, flimsy in appearance and barely large enough to cover the spottail's head. The fish swam around the inlet pipe. I told Sara to stop reeling. Immediate action was called for. I waded in, took the leader in hand, and gently eased the fish up on shore.

I had to be gentle, for the spottail, about 12 pounds or so, was held by one long-shank Eagle Claw size 6 hook, intended for spot. Fortunately, the hook had curled around the fish's lip and Sara had battled the red drum easily enough to keep the hook from pulling out. I put the fish on a stringer, grabbed my camera and tagging equipment, and tagged the fish with a bright yellow plastic strip. My wife, Patricia, arrived just in time to take a picture of us as we were about to release Sara's first spottail.

To my little girl's credit, not a tear was shed, but there was some disappointment that we had not kept the fish. I explained that since we were not cooking this weekend, it would be better to let someone else catch the fish, as happened a year later. Of course, none of Sara's teachers and friends at school believed her fish story—until a letter from Don Hammond of the South Carolina Wildlife and Marine Resources Department confirmed the re-catching of Sara's tagged fish almost a year later.

As for that Kiawah Island salt pond, access to it is usually limited to property owners, but there are other salt ponds along the Carolina and Georgia coasts that can provide excellent fishing for those who can find them. Fishermen who know about them will no doubt keep the secret to themselves. Kiawah's secret is a happy memory for father and daughter.

Hunting Island: Surf Blues, Lagoon Spot, and Hungry Raccoons

One of the favorite locations for photographers attempting to capture the spirit of the South Carolina coast is an old and weathered dead tree that still stands in the surf at Hunting Island State Park. When plantation owners first began fishing the surf of the Carolina coast, they discovered that artificial reefs, even in the surf, quickly attracted sheepshead and red drum, for a basic principle of coastal fishing is that if there is cover for baitfish and crustacea, bigger fish will soon be around to dine on them. Thus the barkless, smooth, and silvery trees still left at Hunting Island attract fish as well as fishermen. Besides, they are "scenic" on coastal barrier islands where the surfline, at least at high tide, shows little variation.

My younger son was seven years old the first time we fished Hunting Island's surf, pulling in blues and catfish on a brisk October day. The suck of wet sand under our bare feet and the splash of still warm saltwater on our legs made the usually static art of waiting for a bite a constantly changing experience. With patience, we might have hooked some spotted sea trout and red drum, especially if we had the time to inspect the surf at low tide to see where the holes and sloughs were. But as on many another modestly successful fishing trip, we had to take advantage of what was biting when we had a last few hours of fishing time late on a Friday afternoon. Three blues for dinner were enough reward and the saltwater catfish provided a little extra interest.

We were visiting the island and its state park at the invitation of Charles Moore of the Marine Resources Division of the South Carolina Wildlife and Marine Resources Department. Moore is a persistently hard worker in getting out booklets and pamphlets on sharks, spadefish, and every other saltwater gamefish on the South Carolina coast, to say nothing of shrimp, oysters, clams, and even whelks, all eminently harvestable and edible. Moore also has a keen sense of fun when it comes to the outdoors, and it was he who tipped us off on the scavenging raccoons of the island who put on a post-midnight show around the garbage cans behind the comfortable cottages available for rental by the public.

When my then four-year-old daughter insisted that she also be taken fishing, I thought that the lagoon on the other side of the island might be more congenial. No waves to contend with there, so Sara might be able to pull in a fish or two once Dad

The lagoon at Hunting Island provides easy spot fishing for old and young anglers.

had made an easy cast with a one-ounce sinker and two small hooks baited with pieces of worm.

We drove back by the small bridge connecting the island to the mainland, bought some worms at a conveniently located (right on the marsh) bait shop, and made our way, armed with bug spray, to the lagoon. (For anyone going to a barrier island for a fishing trip it is probably a good idea to bring some shrimp or freshly caught and salted mullet along on ice for bait in case no bait shop is handy—a throw net, of course, comes in even handier.) The tide was almost high in the lagoon and the spot were in, too, following their October instinct to provide sport even for the newest of Carolina anglers, in this case, my daughter. A few other local anglers had come to the island via its connecting bridge and parked their cars near the lagoon. Armed with a variety of freshwater tackle, all were pulling in the spot, sometimes two at a time.

One of the advantages of the state parks of our Southeast coast is that many of the most scenic fishing spots are still just that, beautiful places that man may visit and fish, but places still unmarked by boardwalks and buildings. The cries of semitropical birds echoed among the cypresses, a breeze kept the insects at bay, and my daughter proudly held up her first fish, caught all by herself, against the background of an island lagoon. Such places are, thank goodness, still not rare all along the Southeast coast.

Beaufort: The Eel and Cobia Man

"It was a brave man who first ate an oyster" or words to that effect might well be applied to the discovery—the Latin word is *inventio*—that the wriggling, slimy, serpentine eel was as fine a bait as one could use for cobia, the toughest fighting and best eating fish on our coast. We don't know who ate that first oyster, so we can't thank him for giving us the courage to slurp up those shellfish cold and succulent or even steaming hot. But we do know the South Carolinian who was innovative enough to discover that eels made great cobia bait. Beaufort native Jack Skinner didn't keep it a secret either.

Most fishermen on the lower part of the South Carolina coast

133

will agree that a live eel is the best bait to use on a big cobia. Big for a cobia may be 71 pounds, like the one Dell Skinner caught one day when she got after her husband, Jack, to take her fishing in Port Royal Sound south of Beaufort. The sound is formed by the confluence of the Broad and Beaufort rivers and no man has taken more cobia from this beautiful body of water than Jack Skinner.

One fine spring day about 40 years ago, Skinner was fishing by the Broad River Bridge and he ran out of live black seabass, the usual bait for cobia at that time. (He was re-telling the story to an old friend, Ray Scribner, and a pair of visiting anglers. Despite surgery that had removed a lung ravaged by cancer, Skinner brightened to his task of recalling every delicious moment of a few of his many encounters with cobia on the rivers, sounds, and ocean of his beloved Low Country.) His eyes lighted up as he remembered a big cobia swimming near the surface near his boat and him out of live baits—except for some eels that were in a minnow trap he happened to have on board.

"I had fished up my blackfish. Well, now, cobia will bite about everything else. Why not an eel? I had to figure out some way to get the eel on the hook. I took my handkerchief and by the time I got through wrestling with him to where I thought he'd stay on the hook, I done took off all the slime." Meanwhile, that cobia was cruising toward his boat again.

"Yonder he comes, his tail and dorsal fin doing like this." Skinner held out his hand from his bed and demonstrated the excited movements of the big cobia. "Well, he took it like he had good sense, the first one (eel bait) I ever threw."

The rest is a chapter of Carolina fishing. While Skinner would fish for weeks at a time without seeing anyone else fishing on the river or sound, there may be 50 or 60 boats out there now on a May weekend fishing the "Cobia Hole." Skinner and charter boat skipper Ray Scribner have a good laugh here, for the "Cobia Hole" is not the best spot for their favorite fish.

As Skinner looked back on four decades of cobia fishing, he recalled the patience it took. "If I can't get him today, I'll get him tomorrow" was his attitude. Eleven cobia in a little boat and a northeast wind whipping up the sound was just one of his most vivid memories. He fondly recalled the 71-pound cobia his wife caught on a day when his back was bothering him so badly that he felt he couldn't get out of bed. That monster was hooked at low water and as Dell fought the fish their boat drifted back up the river behind the rifle range at the Marine Corps Parris Island training facility. The marines came out in a boat to run him off, but Skinner said he wasn't going to turn loose a fish that big. They ceased firing until the lady could get the fish to the boat where Skinner gaffed it, a fish bigger than any he had ever taken. He noted that his wife wanted him to fight the fish when she grew tired, but he refused, saying "No one asked you to come fishing today."

Skinner and his wife would drive from Beaufort up the coast to Georgetown just to fish for eels. Actually he was trapping them, using minnow traps, some shrimp squashed down with his foot into the wire of the trap. At the docks of the Gulf Auto Marine, just up the bay from R.Y. Cathou's fish house, the Skinners would take enough eels to sell for bait for the whole week. Why did he go to Georgetown for eels? "I knew the country," he responded. "I knew where the damn eels were."

Skinner also knew where the cobia were and how to catch them—with his favorite bait.

Parris Island: When the Wampus Comes to Trunkett

We are in an estuary near Parris Island, South Carolina. As retired Marine Corps officer Ray Scribner maneuvers his creek boat through an unmarked channel only a veteran fisherman could find, the vibrantly pure air of a sunny November day makes us glad that we had awakened at four in the morning for the drive to Beaufort and a day of creek fishing, although in the pre-dawn dark and cold we had had a few second thoughts. The kings are still running offshore. April through October, Paradise Pier at Hunting Island is where Scribner docks his charter boat "The Warrior." He heads through the inlet between Hunting Island and Fripp Island to fish the reefs and wrecks off these islands and Hilton Head to the south. But today is for fun, and fun for Scribner in November means bass (spottail bass or red drum) and trout (spotted sea trout or "winter" trout, another member of the drum family and probably the prettiest and best eating, too).

The tide has nearly fallen out of our guide's favorite creek, but we sneak up to a turn in the bank where a dead tree lies half in the water. Two fishermen from Parris Island are anchored within casting distance of the tree. As we slide to a stop, one of them is reeling in a splashing bass, quickly followed by a small sheepshead hooked by his companion. They've been out since dawn and the bottom of their small boat has the evidence, three dozen spottails averaging a few pounds apiece. Scribner flips a live shrimp toward the fallen tree, but misses our only strike before the water goes slack. Our guide decides to head back toward the creek mouth which empties into the Beaufort River.

Tom Owens, a friend of ours who visits from Illinois every fall, hooks a small trout on a white plastic grub at our next stop, a few hundred yards up another creek, but the fishing is still slow. We anchor at a creek mouth next to an oyster bank. Across the shell banks, three men are harvesting oysters by hand, but we look on the oyster banks as an attractor for bass and trout. It's just before noon, the water is clear and flat, and the tide is starting to move back in. So are the fish. I miss a strike on a Mirrolure, Owens ties into another sparkling trout, and Scribner sets the hook on his first bass of the day. His patience and knowledge of the waters have paid off. If we had only left at two in the morning rather than four, we would have taken a good catch in his first choice of spots, too. But that's the choice a fisherman often has to make, a few hours more sleep, or a few hours more of prime fishing. Time and tide—and fish—wait for no man.

A small cabin cruiser comes in off the river, barely scraping across the shell banks farther out from where we are fishing. It is Waldo Phinney, one of the senior South Carolina charter boat skippers, fishing today for fun with live shrimp for trout and bass. We exchange comments on the fishing as Phinney and a friend anchor a bit closer to the creekmouth. Our luck holds as I set the hook of a green "Swimmin' Grub" on what turns out to be a three-pound spottail bass that makes my light rod bend and tests the smoothness of the drag on my reel. (I hereby make a public confession of my stubbornness; if I had fished with live shrimp, as Scribner did, I would have caught more fish. But that's my—or any angler's—decision.)

Scribner recites the litany of the seasons for us as an afternoon breeze begins to pick up. "Offshore we have good bottom fishing all year around, if you can get offshore: seabass, grouper (his secret bait is amberjack and like many other fishermen along the coast he is a firm believer in using bait scents to perk up jaded appetites down on the ocean bottom) and snapper. In the spring the big bluefish show up early and I get to use all those lures that I bought the season before that didn't work on the kings. The blues will hit anything. Then it's kings, cobia, barracuda, and amberjack over the reefs until the fall."

Later he will show me how he artfully rigs heavy monofilament or wire to fish live eels for cobia or kings. Scribner is proud of the good results from "fish aggregation devices," basically mid-water anchored floats that attract schools of baitfish followed naturally by hungry gamefish. "Everybody who fishes regularly out of Fripp Inlet pitched in to put them together and get them set out there. They do work." He urges us to check with Mel Bell of the South Carolina Wildlife and Marine Resources Department for details. I mention that Bell had given a presentation on artificial reefs to the college students at our annual intercollegiate fishing match and seminar. Scribner promises to come up for the 1986 Invitational with a bunch of good stories and true information to delight students and other anglers. He kept his word.

Scribner's best story involves a young black man whose language still retained some of the phrases of the original French settlers of the Beaufort area. His name was Isaac Cohen, "Ike Coin" to his friends and neighbors, and the year was 1966 or so. Cohen inquired about an old boat Scribner had just bought: "That your bateau, mon?" When Scribner allowed that it was indeed his boat, his interlocutor made a proposition: "What say we take a grainge (fish spear) and go strike (spear) some trute (trout), mon?" In the still of that night they headed out to "Trunkett" (Trenchards) Inlet.

Scribner was nervous. Over the flats and the dead calm water came the sound of what he insists were voodoo drums echoing through the night. On the water, Scribner's guide was patient and optimistic. "We strike trute when wampus comes, mon." When Scribner asked how he would know when the "wampus" came, his guide, as guides will do, reassured him. "Hey, mon, when wampus he come, you know about it." There was a huge splash audible but unseen a few hundred yards away and Cohen began knocking his fish spear against the side of the boat. He was calling the wampus. Then just off the starboard side the water erupted. "I just about jumped out of the bateau." The wampus was a porpoise! Cohen had learned to attract the porpoises to the boat, Scribner swears, by rapping with the fish spear against the side of the boat. Three porpoises came in, one on each side in front of the boat and one in deep water. The deep-water wampus would herd the trout toward the other two and they would grab some but herd most of the trout toward the boat. Now and then the guide would throw one of his close-in partners a trout, and the three wampus—like Latin fourth declension nouns, e.g. "spiritus," the plural and singular are identical in the nominative case in Cohen's language although Scribner uses the Anglicized form "wampuses"—would rotate so one would be working and two eating.

"It was an obvious case of teamwork," Scribner recalls. "Ike was striking 'trute' like crazy with the 'grainge' and all I was doing was watching with my mouth open, because I ain't never seen nothing like this before. . . . I don't blame you if you don't believe me, but I saw it." Since that first encounter with the wampus, Scribner testifies that he has called porpoises to his boat on many a trout-gigging trip. "You hear the wampuses, you call them to the boat, they get to eat, you get to eat."

Scribner has seen fishing pressure increase tremendously in the sounds and off the coast. It's part of the price of living on the coast when living here has become popular. But he rails against trawlers in the rivers and sounds. "They come in for three days for shrimp and they wipe out the fishing and mess up the bottom. And when a study group recommended that trawling nets be banned in the sound, the group was dismantled." Scribner shakes his head as we count our catch, seven spottail bass and three winter trout. It used to be better, but it's still pretty nice, especially with a guide who knows how to tell a true tale, or at least a good one. Or as Vincent Zichello would say, *"Se non e vero, e ben trovato."*

Hilton Head Island: A Tale of Two Fishermen

Dean Poucher was a witness that first year, 1967, out toward the Gulf Stream, some 70 miles from shore, when South Carolina anglers first began tangling with blue marlin. He would have been taking pictures of Virginia Pingree as she whipped the Palmetto state's first big billfish, but he had to work elsewhere

Author Dean Poucher took this speckled trout on a soft plastic-tailed grub while fishing in a creek near Hilton Head Island.

Photo by Ted Borg, courtesy of *South Carolina Wildlife*

that day. Later that summer he made sure his work included going out on those pioneering billfish trips and writing about them. Marlin fishing has slowed since those glory days of the late '60s—exploring the moon was not the only frontier back then— and so has one of Hilton Head Island's most famous anglers, Dean Poucher. Four back operations haven't succeeded in making an ordinary offshore trip fun. With all his writing and picture taking in those days, he never got to hook a blue marlin. "Even back then I couldn't afford the price of 300 gallons of diesel fuel." Today he would be happy just to get out after some spotted sea trout on Broad Creek.

Millions of Americans know the sportfishing boats at Hilton Head's Harbour Town only as the background to "The Heritage," an important professional golf tournament. Dean Poucher remembers the way it used to be, back in the pioneer days of billfishing in South Carolina, when the Sea Pines fishing tournament almost always meant lots of big blue marlin. Sad to say, that was less than 20 years ago.

Another man who remembers is Lem Winesett, whose jon boat is a familiar sight to anglers fishing the Intracoastal Waterway and Skull Creek out to Port Royal Sound at the north end of Hilton Head. "There are millions of acres of water there and there's no substitute for getting out there and looking for the trout." Winesett used to edit and publish the *Horry Herald* and before that saw his newspaper in Loris, South Carolina, lost in a card game—not by him, but do ask him to tell the story. He also remembers how trout fishing used to be near his Hilton Head home: "In the early '70s you could catch trout year round and big trout in the fall. But ever since that big freeze we had about five years ago fishing has been sporadic. Perhaps it's coming back now, but when I first started fishing the Intracoastal and those areas it was really good."

Winesett is a patient fisherman. He has his boat rigged so that he can drop an anchor from the bow without leaving his seat by the motor. That's an especially convenient arrangement for someone who is willing to spend a half a day patiently trying one shell bank or creek mouth after another. He eases his boat to a spot, exercising care not to run it over a potential school of feeding trout. Winesett drops the anchor, and starts casting. His Mirrolures, plastic plugs with three treble hooks, look very much the same, not the bright factory blends of white, yellow, and red, perhaps with spots, but day-glo reds and oranges and limes that he applies with cans of spray paint.

He casts to the bank next to the weeds, lets the lure sink, and works the plug slowly with the current, occasionally twitching it. Winesett's rods look almost as old as the man who wields them. He concentrates on that slight touch that is a winter trout swallowing a swimming lure. And in a lull in the fishing he tells stories on himself. Like the time he checked his line inside his home but in the chill of early morning found the old monofilament snapping on fish after fish. No one to blame but himself; he shakes his head with a smile as he tells of those five pounders he missed.

Four or five casts come up empty and he moves his boat to another location. Same procedure: cast, reel slowly, flip the wrist, wait, watch, feel. No hits. Up anchor.

This time he decides to troll along a shell bank. He ties a green plastic grub with bright red lead head on in place of the Mirrolure and throttles his motor way down. Cast, close the bail of his spinning reel—an old open-faced reel that looks like it has been banged around for a decade or more—and let that lure hum down next to the shell bank. Twitch, twitch, hit, snap, set the hook. Once again, Winesett's patience pays off.

Poucher's memories extend past those pioneering battles with billfish, through memorable cobia, dolphin, and kings, to the simple pleasures of a morning's trout fishing in the sheltered waters behind Hilton Head Island, simple pleasures that this veteran outdoor writer appreciates even more now because his back problems have prevented him from enjoying them.

But he has his special memories, particularly of one golden morning in the Gulf Stream when a sea of sargassum pollenated so that it seemed that their boat, the "Roulette," had just then "entered the pearly gates of the New Jerusalem itself. . . . One minute fishermen were hurrying about their tasks and the next they were transfixed as the glorious rays of the sun caught a solid, shimmering sheet of gold dust that paved the indigo undulating surface as far as the eye could see."

It is good that we still have the eyes of men like Dean Poucher and Lem Winesett who can look into the past and make us think about the future, even as so many others cannot look beyond the present and the short-term, quick-profit future.

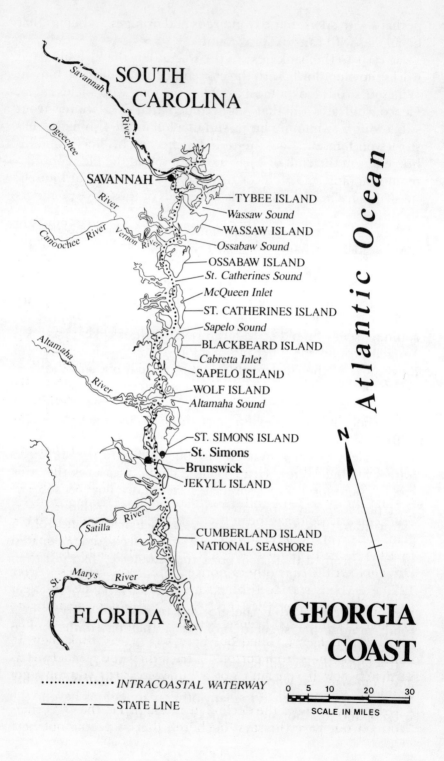

SOUTH
CAROLINA

Savannah River

Ogeechee River

SAVANNAH

TYBEE ISLAND
Wassaw Sound
WASSAW ISLAND
Ossabaw Sound
OSSABAW ISLAND
St. Catherines Sound
McQueen Inlet
ST. CATHERINES ISLAND
Sapelo Sound
BLACKBEARD ISLAND
Cabretta Inlet
SAPELO ISLAND
WOLF ISLAND
Altamaha Sound
ST. SIMONS ISLAND
St. Simons
Brunswick
JEKYLL ISLAND

CUMBERLAND ISLAND
NATIONAL SEASHORE

Canoochee River

Vernon River

Altamaha River

Satilla River

St. Marys River

FLORIDA

Atlantic Ocean

N

GEORGIA
COAST

············· *INTRACOASTAL WATERWAY*
———— - —— STATE LINE

0   5   10   20   30
SCALE IN MILES

19

Georgia

The Ogeechee River:
Five Redbreast on a Beargrass Stringer

The fish camp was less than an hour from Savannah but light years away. Around the ramp there were signs of commercial fishing, big nets and floats. The little creek that we were putting our boat into had barely enough water for a flat-bottomed boat with two passengers and a 25-horsepower motor. On the river, we found an older couple (I believe they said they had driven out from Savannah) flipping their cane poles and cricket baits up against a log, with a few fat redbreast to show for it. The only noise once we cut our engine was the sound of birds chirping in the delight of clean air and bright May sunshine. The water was clear, too, and as the day grew warmer it would tempt any fisherman with a bit of the boy in him to strip to his shorts and take the plunge.

Vereen Driggers, resident historian of the rustic but romantically named Safari Fish Camp, was still waiting for his first Ogeechee River sturgeon of the season. He had been born in Bryan County in 1914 and started commercial fishing in 1929. Sturgeon and shad had been the mainstay of his catch, with the giant sturgeon the most dramatic product of this winding river. In 1984 he had caught seven, although 1979 was his best year. Driggers recalls that others noticed the good catches: "After 1979 everybody started fishing for sturgeon. . . . The trouble is now that every Tom, Dick, and Harry will go down there and get 'em a commercial license. Shad, sturgeon, catfish. . . . The first net that I ever fished out here was in '29; back then we knitted those nets from cotton . . . back then you take a twenty-yard net; now if you ain't got a hundred yards you ain't got nothing."

Driggers lamented the decline in all the fish in the Ogeechee. "You get out here (he says 'ouchere') there's people out here with telephones and baskets and you call the law enforcement and they ain't got enough of help to put a man out here." (The telephone devices are still used to shock catfish which float to the surface for easy but illegal harvesting.) "Law enforcement on the Ogeechee just doesn't get the help and the nets are strung all the way across the river by part-time fishermen."

When asked about the future of the coastal rivers, Driggers was quick to point out that environmental restrictions have already helped. "They have cleaned out the Savannah River. You used to get oil all over your nets. It's a lot cleaner now, they tell me."

He keeps returning to his theme of supporting the law for everybody's good on the river: "They don't have the proper support, the environmental people don't have the people for law enforcement." As a boat is pulled out of the water, we check the catch: redbreast and bream. Driggers holds one of the fish, the biggest redbreast of the morning for the two anglers who had been fishing with float lines and crickets. The fish is fat, the orange of its belly in bright contrast to its dark upper body. "Back when I started fishing in 1929 we would get a stringer of five

A couple fishes with cane poles in the Ogeechee River on a balmy spring day.

redbreast like this and string them on beargrass stringers and sell 'em for a quarter a stringer . . . if you made two dollars and a half a week you had a big payday. Any way you could make a dollar back then was a dollar."

It would be easy to become melancholy about the decline of fishing in the Ogeechee and other coastal Georgia and Carolina rivers. It is not what it used to be. But on the other hand, far more people than ever before are concerned that the condition of these rivers be maintained or improved. Anyone who has the chance to get out on the Ogeechee—or any river along the Georgia coast—to fish or just ride will probably be on the side of old-timers like Vereen Driggers . . . even if they can't sell redbreast on beargrass stringers anymore.

Ossabaw Sound: From Trout and Flounder to Kings and Cobia

"I see my future offshore," says the skipper of the sportfishing boat as we head down the Vernon River toward Ossabaw Sound. Dr. Paul Ward is a professor at Armstrong State University in Savannah, but he would rather be fishing the rivers around his coastal Georgia home. Striped bass, shad, spotted sea trout, and flounder are among his favorite fish. Still, it's not like it used to be. "I caught but one shad this year and I fished a half dozen times. The shad fishing has gone down very rapidly. Ten years ago I was catching 12 to 16 in a day. It's a combination of several things: silting in of the mouth of the river, overfishing by the commercial people . . . they don't want to cooperate at all."

He gestured at what I perceived to be an idyllic setting. Marsh, clean flowing water, herons wading in the shallows, very few buildings along the edge of the tidal river, with oyster banks still showing above the slowly rising tide. But like so many other saltwater fishermen throughout the Carolinas and Georgia, Ward felt that something was being lost, and quickly at that. "The whole coast of Georgia is going down the drain. It's going to be a strip city from the Florida line to South Carolina and the people are going to crowd into the coastal area and take over all of the Waterway. In 20 years you won't be able to see anything like this."

Our conversation about coastal fishing had begun up toward

the dividing line between freshwater and saltwater, a line that shifts with the tide. Ward was showing us his favorite spots for stripers (winter) and shad (late spring) while describing his recipe for "King Steaks Italiano," king mackerel steaks marinated overnight in Italian salad dressing, popped on a hot grill until seared, seared on the other side until the juices were sealed in, and then cooked on aluminum foil with the rest of the juice from the salad dressing to moisten them, the top being placed over the grill to help bake the steaks. He had also revealed his method for shad baked eight slow hours at 250 degrees in a pan with milk until the bones dissolved. He asked whether South Carolinians ate blackfin tuna. When I responded enthusiastically to both his recipes and the idea of blackfin tuna steaks, Ward talked about why he had moved toward offshore reef fishing.

"I have gotten somewhat frustrated around here," he said with a gesture at the slowly moving river—despite his complaints and the beauty of the late May afternoon there were only two other boats on the water that weekday afternoon. "Because of so many people moving in, there's always someone fishing on the river through the summer and fall months." (That afternoon we would watch dozens of people fishing from the railroad trestle on the Bull River, with some saltwater panfish to show for it.) "My father-in-law takes bluefish, croaker, and whiting from the beaches on Tybee Island. Some people even get winter trout."

Nothing wrong with all that, but far below his expectations. When Ward moved to the Savannah area in the 1960s, fishing was terrific, basically an untouched resource. Like the eighteenth-century American hunters described by St. John Crevecoeur, who moved farther into the wilderness as others moved into their hunting territory, Ward has directed his fishing attention offshore to the manmade reefs off the Georgia coast. "You have to run at least 15 miles offshore to get to really clean water. The reefs have such comparatively small pressure that fishing for black seabass and kings has remained constant, even getting better as the bottom builds up. The state built the first one over a decade ago, but as less money becomes available, fishing clubs and individuals are taking up the slack. We get kings in late spring, cobia, and I've even seen a sailfish at the J Buoy. September has the biggest kings."

We have headed down river on the outgoing tide, and the water

DONALD MILLUS

Professor Paul Ward agrees with the angler pictured, Dr. Lloyd Newberry, that the best of Georgia's coastal angling is in salt water, here inshore for tarpon.

Photo by Wyck Newberry

has now gone slack. The fresh smell of salt marsh in spring has a renewing effect, perhaps somehow on the mind as well as on the body. With the turn of the tide, Ward turns his sport fishing boat, better suited to the reefs than to river fishing, back upstream. Ann Ward, Paul's talented and serene artist wife, smiles as he talks about the fishing in the rivers and offshore. She knows her husband's love of fishing, but she looks out at the tidal river with the eyes of the artist as well. I agree with her unspoken thought: the fishing may not be as great as he remembers it, but this place is still beautiful. The sun is setting behind the marsh grass as we make the last turn back toward the dock. A Georgia coastal river is still a good place to be—quiet, uncrowded, clean, and peaceful.

Sea Islands and Gulf Stream:
"Not Just One River of Fish"

In 1972 Dr. S. Lloyd Newberry fished the Gulf Stream waters off the Georgia coast for the first time. It was almost virgin fishing territory, 75 miles out at sea, a four-hour voyage in ocean waters that "most of the time" were not conducive to long runs in a small boat. "Fishing was better then, but it's still pretty good. I've fished Hatteras, the Florida Keys, and West Palm Beach, and never fished anywhere that was nearly as productive. No one was out there and many rivers of fish were coming together, not just one river of fish. There was no one out there and 70 percent of the time the water was almost too rough for good fishing." It was a young man's game, physically punishing but rewarding, fishing the Gulf Stream far off the Georgia coast.

We were standing in the backyard of his home. Down below us the waters of the Ogeechee River moved by on the incoming tide. The river was flat in the late spring sunshine, but here and there a flipping wave dappled the surface, the product not of wind but of huge schools of menhaden breaking the surface. Out of the main current, in shallow water, a big mullet jumped. Newberry thought about bait and preparing for his offshore jaunts.

"We would start preparing on Thursday night by rigging baits." (Baits meant ballyhoo, mullet, and other smaller fish that would be carefully rigged on wire leaders with stainless steel hooks sharpened to a fine point and colorful artificial skirts—the stuff of which strikes from blue marlin, yellowfin tuna, wahoo, kings, and big bull dolphin are made.) "We would cast off at midnight on Friday, and it would be an hour's run to the open sea, and four hours more to the Gulf Stream." Most of those rides were pounding trips, but 75 miles later in water of a hundred fathoms and more the dawn would frequently be accompanied by billfish and wahoo breaking the surface behind those carefully rigged baits.

"It's still really good because the grounds out there are not fished heavily." No wonder; after a full day of fishing there was the four-hour run back to shore and a late night return to his dock on the river. "It took you two days to recover from the trip, and by then it was time to get ready for the next weekend trip to the Gulf Stream."

The walls of Newberry's study are covered with trophy fish from the productive waters off the Georgia coast and from around the world. Billfish, wahoo, dolphin, and tuna are just the beginning. There is a tarpon there as a reminder of what good inshore fishing can be had at the right time of year. In fact, Newberry admits that he now prefers the contemplative—and more easily reached—pleasures of fishing the Sea Islands of his Georgia coast.

"It's so much more pleasurable. . . ." His voice trails off as he remembers the pounding of those long trips to the Stream. But there is a smile of satisfaction there, too, the recollection of

Dr. Lloyd Newberry took this wahoo far offshore. The wahoo is both a great fighter and outstanding tablefare.

Photo by Wyck Newberry

149

battles prepared for and won. Not that fishing the Sea Islands—Sapelo Island and Cabretta Inlet, plus McQueen Inlet on St. Catherines Island are among his favorite spots—is a walk in the park. The islands must be approached carefully by anglers able to handle a small boat and fend for themselves far removed, at least for half a day, from civilization. Newberry anchors the boat in protected water and walks on the sandbars looking for places where the incoming tide converges in cross currents. In frothy waters sometimes just a few feet deep he fishes with cut mullet or squid—"You can buy a bucket of fresh squid right from the shrimp boats." (Later in the year he and his friends would beach six channel bass that would have totaled over 150 pounds if they had not released the bruisers alive for someone else to enjoy. His rig was a fish finder rig—sliding sinker—with 20-pound test line on a Penn squidding reel and a 10-foot custom-made rod.) He evaluates fishing from the Sea Islands:

"All the beaches are good. The best places to fish are the north or south ends of the islands and that makes it easy to park your boat. The best months are October and November. There are speckled trout there, too, and I've even caught tarpon in the surf, although the best bet is to troll a live mullet or Creek Chub (a plug) in Altamaha Sound in late August."

Newberry is thankful for the islands. "Between the islands given to the state in lieu of taxes and the purchases of the Georgia Nature Conservancy, there are hundreds of miles of shoreline that will stay protected and undeveloped. "We lucked out," he says with a smile, anticipating his next trip to fish Georgia's prized Sea Islands.

Part Three:

Learning to Fish the Southeast Coast

Introduction

I once heard a philosophy professor comment that one can become truly expert on only a limited subject or area of study. An angler who gets lucky and finds out what the fish are hitting on a particular day when no one else can catch fish becomes the master teacher for the day. Other fishermen, even more experienced anglers, will come alongside to inquire about bait or lures. All fishing tackle, in fact, also has its fascination for fishing man, descendant of thousands of generations of tool-making and tool-using men and women, always fascinated by mankind's ingenuity and the fine reels, rods, and lures that have resulted from trial and error. In fishing, one learns from experience and from others. Both nature and the fishermen of the Southeast coast have school open all year long for those who want to learn about fishing here.

20

The Piers

Piers concentrate both fish and fishermen. Contemporary freshwater bass fishing has had volumes written about "structure"—that is, rocks, dropoffs, sandbars, trees and bushes wholly or in part underwater, anything that might provide a hiding place or "cover" for predator or prey. The pier in the ocean is its own structure, attracting bigger fish to feed on smaller fish and crustacea that find a home around the pilings and under the pier. On top, add lights, running water, fish cleaning tables, snack bars, rest rooms, and tackle shops and the piers attract fishermen.

"What's biting today?" is the first question to ask, even if it's by telephone. If the fish were biting earlier in the day, plan to fish at the appropriate time or tide on the morrow. The odds are that if the spot, croaker, bluefish, flounder, sheepshead, kings, or pompano hit yesterday on the early morning tide, barring a drastic change in the weather they will hit today on the same tide.

Pier fishing gives one a place to lean a rod and time both for reflection and to ask questions of other fishermen. Some may not be eager to talk, but basic human friendliness and generosity often lead to the sharing of years of fishing experience. That freshwater outfit you use on the pond or lake back home will be all you need to get started. You may want to take a quick tour of the pier, usually at no charge, just to check on what's biting on what bait. Check also on terminal tackle, buy a package of bloodworms or shrimp for bait along with your pier ticket, and use the same method everyone else who is catching fish is using. While spot, croaker, and pompano are easy to catch when they're running, trout, big flounder, and king mackerel may demand a bit more sophistication in tackle and methods. Remember the old Peace Corps radio ad where the father-in-law tells the son he

The sign in the background on this North Carolina pier brags about tomorrow's fishing, but they were biting today as this flounder angler discovered. The piers are perhaps the best "classroom" for newcomers and visitors who want to learn more about fishing the Southeast coast.

doesn't have to know anything about pocketbooks to join his business: "What's to know? You'll learn." So, too, on the piers, even if you don't yet own a rod and reel. Go out there and see for yourself. At least you won't get seasick.

Pier Notes: I have deliberately avoided listing all the piers of the Southeast coast, although I do mention many of them in the sections on particular areas such as Topsail Island and Myrtle Beach. What I want to avoid is disappointing an angler who reads about a pier that suddenly became part of an "exclusive" condominium development or was subject to the ravages of a winter Northeaster. Chambers of commerce in each area will provide lists of piers, but by far the best bet for the newcomer is to visit the local bait and tackle shop, make a purchase of suitable bait and terminal tackle and get the best possible up-to-date advice on what pier is producing fish this week.

I should add that dress is important for pier fishing: old sneakers, long-sleeved shirt, and pants to prevent sunburn in the summer—you can go to bathing suit for as long as you want to risk a burn—and extra-warm clothes to suit spring, fall, and winter fishing so you don't have to quit due to shivers just when the trout or croaker start to bite.

Pier etiquette demands that one does not fish too close to another person. Obviously, avoid casting your line over another person's, but if it happens a simple "sorry" will do. When the spot or blues are running fast and heavy, a few feet of open rail may be scarce. The Golden Rule usually works wonderfully on the piers of the Southeast coast, and the courteous novice will often learn a lot from experienced anglers with a few polite questions.

21

The Surf

The Southeast coastline from below Cape Hatteras to the barrier islands of the Georgia coast does not feature the dramatic surf found to the north. Only from the barrier islands and the

*The surf near coastal Carolina piers is a good place for
late fall fishing for winter trout (spotted sea trout).*

jetties at some inlets will long rods and large-capacity reels be needed, and even there you can usually do some good fishing with light to medium spinning or baitcasting outfits. All through the summer and early fall one does not even need a pair of waders. Forget the macho image of big surf, tackle only a behemoth could heave, and chest-high waders with a slicker top adding to your stature and expenses. Often enough, a freshwater spinning outfit will do and ultralight tackle can make even a half-pound whiting or a two-pound bluefish feel like a fish worth writing about.

Given an outfit that allows you to toss an ounce or two of lead and a pair of hooks baited with shrimp, cut mullet (small pieces, the fresher the better), or mole crabs (sand fleas), the only extra piece of equipment needed is a sand spike (a rod holder that is sunk into the sand), even if it's homemade from a piece of plastic piping. Check with area tackle shops for likely places, talk to local fishermen, but get down there to the ocean and get a line in the water, whether it is on the Bogue Banks, on Topsail or Bald Head islands, next to the Second Avenue Pier in Myrtle Beach, or on any of the barrier islands of the rest of the South Carolina and Georgia coasts.

Plan to fish the last two hours of the incoming tide and the first two hours of the outgoing for starters. But if you miss the tide and it is dead low, first, look for some holes that are showing at low tide and plan to fish them as the tide comes in, and then harvest some sand fleas for fishing as the tide comes in. Bottom fishing in the surf does not always mean casting beyond the breakers, for that first drop-off, close to the beach, may be where fish such as pompano, croaker, and red drum are feeding.

Standing in the surf early or late on a summer or early fall day will be good for your arches and your soul. If you can learn some spots to fish with bait in your summertime fishing with freshwater tackle, maybe you'll be back in the fall with waders and a light saltwater spinning outfit to fish with artificials for trout, bigger blues, and drum. But even if you don't catch anything, surf fishing our coast is always rewarding. Stay with it long enough, however, and it may well provide the ingredients for some nice fish dinners. There is a definite pleasure in carrying even a modest stringer of fish, much less a cooler with a few tails hanging out, back to your car past the tourists.

22

Inlets and Coastal Rivers

One of the most pleasant tasks a fisherman can set himself is learning to fish the rivers and inlets of the Southeast coast. It is rewarding in itself just scouting out likely places to fish from the bank, whether it is from an abandoned bridge near Savannah, the lagoon behind Hunting Island State Park, one of the docks at the marinas along the Grand Strand, or the shores of the Cape Fear River or New River. Even more fun is to be had with a small boat and motor, 14 feet and 15 horsepower being enough for a lifetime of fishing in our rivers and inlets.

That freshwater outfit will do for starters and the bait shop nearest the launching ramp will usually give you directions to what's the best bet for the season or day. Then it's simply a matter of putting in the time, observing, and asking the right questions. People like Creekman (W.W. Hills) who have won reputations as experienced anglers frequently find themselves followed by fishermen trying to ferret out the professional's favorite trout or flounder hole, but anyone who is catching fish when you are not is a good source of information and example.

Starting out with the suggestion from the local bait shop may put you into fish, but when the fishing slows down, don't be afraid to experiment. On the other hand, waiting for the right tide may be in order. Patience is not only a virtue but a necessity in fishing, for the fish may not bite until the tide gets right, as happened one day when we anchored by a coastal jetty on a fair summer day with the water clean and the winds light. But nothing was biting. Fortunately, our guest was in no hurry on his first saltwater fishing trip. I noted that it would be at least an hour before the tide got right in that particular spot. How did I know? Just by having put in my time there. Still, there were no guarantees, just good possibilities. In this case, as soon as the tide started to fall and the baitfish were herded along the rocks by the current, blues and spottail bass began hitting bait and lures. The educated guess that pays off with great fishing when all else fails is one of the greatest of life's pleasures.

Besides an assortment of light tackle and lures, a camera and a color-illustrated guide to birds are good companions for those inlet and river trips when the fish aren't biting. If you keep at it, there may come a day when you are the lone angler on the bank or bridge or dock or when your boat is the only one at the edge of the marsh and the flounder, trout, spottail, blues, or striped bass hit everything you throw at them. Alone or with others, as the confessional manuals once put it, such days are the reward of the angler who pays his or her dues on our coastal rivers and inlets.

New River Inlet on the North Carolina coast is ideal for small-boat fishing, as well as for fishing from the banks.

23

Headboats and Charter Boats

Some of the crew members on our coastal headboats are giving fishing lessons on the way out through the inlets of the Carolinas and Georgia. The lesson is brief: first-time anglers are shown how to hold a boat rod, how to hold the line while taking the reel out of gear, and how to get the sinker and two baited hooks to the bottom without tangling up. The rest is self-taught: if you wait too long to strike when the fish bites, you are punished with a cleaned hook. Strike quickly enough (but not too quickly) and you are rewarded with a battling grouper, trigger fish, silver snapper, or more commonly, one or two half-pound black seabass, typical fare on many half-day boats.

Headboats are so-called not because of any facilities on board, but because they take individual anglers or fares at a fixed price per person or "head." Those half-day trips are a good place to start, to find out if all your systems are ready for the test of a whole day at sea. (See Avoiding Seasickness.) The real test of man-(and woman-)hood, however, is the all-day offshore trip. If you don't mind the sight of cutfish and smell of the exhaust, hang out at the stern and watch the crew cutting bait and filleting fresh-caught sea perch for cut bait. Take time to observe how a few clever mates will fish whole live baits for kings and other prowling top-water gamefish, while the paying passengers concentrate on bottomfishing.

Bait and tackle are included in the fare, which ranges from under $20 for a half-day trip for blackfish to $50 or more for a full day of bottomfishing up to 60 miles and more offshore. Especially during the summer months and on early fall weekends, boats can be very crowded. Some less-crowded trips go overnight out toward the Gulf Stream and may last up to 24 hours. Reservations and fares of $100 or more apply for these special trips.

Aside from using the basic anti-motion sickness prevention methods, wear sneakers, old clothes (including a long-sleeved shirt and hat to keep your skin from being burned red on a blazing summer day), and bring a towel for your hands unless you want to pay a young pirate a buck for a quarter towel. Pack your picnic lunch in a cardboard box or heavy "paper sack" and

160

Headboat anglers sometimes fish elbow to elbow, but there are good stringers of fish to show for it.

plan to buy your cold drinks on board. Bring a cooler or two—you'll usually have to leave them in the car lest the boat deck get too crowded—in case the fishing is super. Don't leave your fish on deck in the sun for more than a few minutes after you catch them. Get them on a stringer and have the mate put them in the boat's cooler. Especially good stringers may be hung up for show and tell as the boat docks, while both passengers and crew take pleasure in the admiring comments from spectators at the dock.

Charter Boats

There's nothing like having the boat to yourself, especially with an experienced skipper and guide at the wheel, a clever mate to rig tackle and coach the first-time fisherman, and all the latest electronic fish-finding equipment to put you over the fish with fine tackle in top condition to fish with. All these conditions should hold if you charter a sportfishing boat from the many ports along the North Carolina, South Carolina, and Georgia coasts.

Charters may be for a half-day or full-day trip. Possibilities range from bottomfishing for black seabass through reef-fishing for spadefish, trolling for kings or Spanish mackerel (the most common type of charter along our coast), and live-bait fishing for cobia, to offshore bottomfishing for grouper and snapper to trolling for billfish and dolphin far offshore. Monster shark fishing is another popular charter that need not be terribly expensive, for big sharks may be caught surprisingly close to the mouths of Southeast coastal inlets. Sharkfishing, in fact, may be the best possibility for anyone hoping to set an all-tackle fishing record off the Carolina or Georgia coasts.

Costs vary, depending on how far the skipper has to travel to find the fish and how much bait will be used. For example, a half-day charter for Spanish mackerel which required no freshly rigged baits cost less than $200 for a group of six anglers in 1985, while a billfish expedition on an air-conditioned fishing yacht that had to sail 60 to 70 miles from the dock at Georgetown, South Carolina, would have cost some $900. Up at Morehead City, North Carolina, with the Gulf Stream closer, the trip costs the skipper less. There is some room for bargaining, but remember that with the cost of fuel, insurance, and bait high no one is getting rich in the charter business. Ask around with some comparison shopping. Personal recommendations are a good place to start.

Incidentally, even if you own your own boat, a charter may be a good investment in learning how to fish. Slow trolling for king mackerel, perfected by the fishermen of the North Carolina coast, is best learned firsthand. Thus, chartering a good slow troller for the day is a good way to learn how to fish, particularly if you plan to enter one of our big money tournaments.

Check with the captain on whether you should bring food and drinks. Follow the suggestions for dress and diet as suggested for headboats, and remember that the captain and crew want nothing more than to put you into some great fishing so that you will come back to charter their boat again. In the Northeast many charter boats keep the fish caught—you pay for the fun of fishing—but on the Southeast coast the fish generally belong to the people who charter the boat. Check with the captain before going out so there are no misunderstandings. It's also a good idea to call ahead the night before to check on the weather. If the wind has been blowing northeast at 20 to 25 knots for a few days, it might be wise to postpone your charter to another week.

Even though you have paid for the trip, remember that the captain is the boss. Few things are worse for a good-natured skipper than to have to deal with a bunch of drunks, especially if the weather is bad and the fishing slow. Best wait until afternoon to have that first beer and not ruin the trip for your fellow anglers. Better still, wait until you're home to start the cocktail hour. If you're driving, you'll be tired enough from a day at sea without having to contend with the effects of alcohol, even if you drink moderately.

Many charter boat crews will clean your catch for free, but tips for the crew are expected, especially if the service is attentive and helpful. Ten percent is a reasonable figure; if you can't afford to tip, you shouldn't charter a boat.

If you are an experienced fisherman, make it clear to the skipper that you don't want to reel in someone else's fish. A few of the younger skippers have no idea of the traditional sportfishing concept of hooking and playing a fish from beginning to end. On the other hand, if you are just out for fun and want to make sure that you put a few king mackerel in the boat, let the crew set the hook and hand the rod to one of the members of your party for the fight. Your intentions on this should be made clear to the skipper before sailing, as well as your plans for using any fish caught. For example, if you do hook a fish that you don't plan to eat or mount, whether it's a billfish, shark, or amberjack, insist that it be released after being fought to the boat. After all, you are paying for the trip. Bring a camera to record the big moment.

A well-planned charter trip with an experienced skipper in good weather can be an absolute delight. Just remember that the captain can't control the weather and that the fish aren't always hungry. The odds are in your favor, however, and a charter trip on one of our Southeast coast sportfishing boats may provide a lifetime of memories. For the women and children it may be a great introduction to the fun of fishing which, fortunately, is no longer just a man's world.

For information on charter boats, check the state information

163

sources in the appendix of this book. Some national and most regional outdoor publications will have some charter boat advertising. Local tackle shops often have free fishing weeklies that will contain advertising for charter boats. Even better, when you visit the coast walk down to the charter boat docks late in the afternoon and see which captain has produced fish for his customers. Remember, there are no guarantees: today's great—or poor—fishing may not be repeated on the morrow.

Some Notes on Avoiding Seasickness: I am indebted to Dr. Douglas Nelson of the Marine Science Department at U.S.C.–Coastal Carolina College, to Nancy Owens, R.N., and to my own occasional miseries at sea, for the following suggestions to help prevent or diminish the effects of seasickness. They are tested by experience, but seasickness is like life: There are no guarantees, and when it's bad, it's miserable.

If there were a button to be pressed to end it all for the person afflicted with that brand of motion sickness called seasickness, there would be many more burials at sea. The human body, particularly the stomach and brain, was not designed for life on a tossing deck. Toss the body around, disturb the equilibrium of the inner ear at regular or irregular intervals and you risk the danger of having the brain sending contradictory messages to various systems, including the stomach. Add diesel fumes, the smell of bait, a hangover from the day before, or even a greasy breakfast topped off by too much black coffee and conditions are perfect for a trip to the rail followed by a day below decks wishing the trip or the world would end, with no preference as to which came first.

Avoid partying the night before, get a good night's sleep, eat a normal breakfast preferably with pancakes (low in acid and animal fats) rather than breakfast meat and eggs, drink no orange juice and no more coffee than normal, and you have a good start. If you are not sure how your sealegs are, take two motion sickness preventative pills, following directions, before sailing. (Some people prefer behind-the-ear patches, but try pills such as Dramamine, following directions, first, for the patches make some people very sleepy.) Remember that it's better to be safe than sorry, although I have taken Dramamine out in the ocean after I starting feeling queasy and still managed to save the day—and my breakfast. Usually (and unfortunately) that's too late.

Stay away from the boat's exhaust, try to get fresh air, and avoid seasick people, for seasickness is in good part mental and thus spreads quickly. (One headboat mate told me that on a calm day in mid-summer it was so hot that there was no breeze on a Gulf Stream trip: once one person got sick, and blatantly over-the-rail so, half the other 80 passengers followed suit.) Lying down in an air-conditioned cabin can give some relief, but taking too long in the head or trying to read or to tie rigs in a closed cabin can trigger nausea.

Despite all precautions, you still may feel sick on your first deep-sea trip. Don't panic, as the guidebook says. If you can stay on your feet, stay at the rail and watch the horizon—anything to distract the body from its rocking environment. Lying down in the fresh air helped me on occasion, but lying down in a warm cabin can be disastrous for someone who is already feeling queasy. The head (toilet or rest room) is not a good place to be sick;

Dr. Bill Delia of Conway, South Carolina had to fight off seasickness to boat this bluefish near the Ten Mile Reef.

better lean over the rail and gulp fresh air in after you lose your breakfast. If four hours have elapsed since your last dosage of pills, repeat the dose with a small sip of water. Take no food or beverage other than water, and that in small sips only, until four "queasy-free" hours have passed. Don't take alcoholic beverages.

Don't go on your first deep-sea trip if the weather is marginal, say winds of over 15 m.p.h. and more than a 30 percent chance of rain. If the captain ever tells you it will be rough out there, even though the water looks calm next to the dock, get off and cut your losses. There will always come a nicer day to try your sealegs for the first time.

The last piece of advice is particularly pertinent for youngsters. If the little guy or girl becomes seasick on a half day trip in good weather, wait a year or two before taking him or her out for a full day. Then make sure that the weather report is not just good, but excellent. There's a lot of good fishing from our coastal piers with no seasickness. But if you must go out on what occasionally is called the "frantic Atlantic," follow the above advice and improve your chances of being able to fish and enjoy a day at sea.

24

Buying Your First—or Last— Fishing Outfit

I think the movie character's name was Murray. "You can never have too many eagles," was his memorable line. He was talking about collecting wooden eagles, but fishermen are notorious collectors, too. They collect rods and reels, testing the patience of their wives as they look for another graphite or split bamboo rod to go with the latest computer-designed reel from American, Japanese, German, or Swedish craftsmen.

Although it is impossible to stop after the first one, the truth is that one good fishing outfit can give five or ten years of pleasure, and possibly more. A closet full of tackle is of no use without spending the time on the water. Knowledge, persistence, and careful observing are more important in fishing. Still, that new graphite rod or magnetic reel feels so good and works so fine. Choosing one's first fishing outfit is as important as choosing one's first love, but advice is probably more useful in the former case.

If I had to select one outfit to cover the greatest number of fishing possibilities along the Carolina and Georgia coasts, I would choose a one-piece, seven-foot, medium-action spinning rod, preferably graphite, but glass will do nicely, two-piece if I were planning to travel with it much. A spinning reel (ABU-Garcia, Penn, Shimano, Ryobi, Daiwa, and Zebco are all trustworthy brands) that can hold 200 yards of 12-pound test monofilament line would go with it. Brand names for the rod? Shakespeare (the "Ugly Stick"), Ryobi, Daiwa, ABU-Garcia, Fenwick, and Berkley are always dependable. Prefer guides that are corrosion resistant, and rinse the rod and oil the reel after each use. Have the reel cleaned annually.

The above outfit can be used in the lakes, ponds, and freshwater rivers of our three-state region, as well as for inlet and jetty fishing. Off the beaches, in good weather, one can throw a lure with it for bluefish or use a bottom rig for pompano. On the piers it is a good trout rod and it will do for flounder. Keep it as a bait-catching outfit for offshore fishing and watch everyone get envious when you tie into a five-pound dolphin in the Gulf Stream while all they have is winch-sized tackle.

For those who are fishing only the surf along the Carolina and Georgia coasts, an eight-foot, two-piece medium to stiff action rod that can throw two or three ounces of pyramid sinker along with a couple pieces of cut mullet is an ideal first outfit. This is a great combination for bigger blues and red drum or trout. It is also a good pier rod and with smaller hooks and sinkers will still allow you to enjoy fishing for spot, croaker, flounder, and blues. A two-ounce lure such as the Hopkins or even a lighter Mirrolure plug should sail on this outfit with 12-pound test monofilament. This is not a great boat rod, but it can be used for live-bait fishing from your own boat or from a headboat if you don't have another outfit. Brand names for rods and reels are mentioned above.

Either of the above outfits will let you enjoy fishing and put you out there on the beach or pier where you can learn more by experience. If the bug continues to bite, as Nelson Bryant puts it, and Santa Claus owes you a really nice gift, a one-piece eight-foot medium action baitcasting rod with a long (at least three feet) cork grip and a fine baitcasting reel such as the Ambassadeur may be your next choice. This outfit is a classic for fishing sand fleas (mole crabs), bloodworms, or cut mullet in the surf; for casting Mirrolures for trout or Hopkins jigs for blues; for fishing grubs for trout or trolling mud minnows for flounder; for fishing live bait or artificials for striped bass, or for trolling for shad.

I should close with a note about two reels, one made in the United States, the other made in Sweden. Both are "conventional" or rotating spool reels as opposed to "spinning" or fixed spool reels where a rotating bail puts line on a spool. They are the Penn reel and the Ambassadeur. I own a number of both of them and have never discarded any of them. They are a little more expensive, but as the television commercial used to put it (why did they kill it?) "darn well worth it." I will not be surprised to see Japanese manufacturers such as Daiwa and Ryobi challenging Penn and ABU-Garcia (the importers of the Ambassadeur) in the conventional reel market, for their products are also impressive. The bottom line for the angler is that there is more fine fishing tackle available than ever before at reasonable prices.

For those who don't fish, but want to buy an outfit for a youngster, the Zebco closed-faced spinning reel with rod to match is ideal if the youngster will be fishing mostly in fresh water. Practical, serviceable, kid-proof (well, almost), some Zebco 33's have endured a decade or two of hard use and still go fishing regularly around the Carolinas and Georgia. Get a five-foot inexpensive glass rod to go with it and let the youngster get out and learn to fish.

A cane pole, a package of hooks, an improvised cork float, and a few pieces of cut bait can also provide anyone who has never fished before with the equipment to catch a dinner from a coastal creek. The fish may not be big, but Bryant says, "I'll fish for minnows in a puddle if nothing else is biting." Cane pole or sophisticated tackle, it's what you do with it that counts.

Acquiring Tackle: Travel Light

Did you ever wonder what your tackle does in the box between fishing trips? It multiplies of course, even while your hooks are rusting. There's no substitute, though, for having the right size hook when the fish are biting. For instance, on an otherwise slow day you observe that boats anchored in the mouth of the inlet are pulling in spot two at a time and you realize that the smallest hook you have in your box is a much-too-large size 1/0. Still, experts estimate that 40 to 50 percent of the tackle bought in this country is never used. Travel light!

There are some other suggestions I would like to make about buying tackle. First of all, buy brand-name monofilament. Ande, DuPont's "Stren" or "Prime," Berkley's "Trilene," Cortland, Maxima, and Shakespeare are all brands of line that experienced fishermen rely on, with each one having his preferences. Although I have landed fish on monofilament that has been on a reel for three years, sun and the passage of time will weaken line. A fresh spool of line, with exactly enough to fill the reel, makes casting, as well as landing fish, that much easier. On the other hand, changing line before your first fishing trip of the spring is not essential unless you are a tournament fisherman. One line-company executive admitted to me that the "change line every spring" theory helped sales immensely, but that fishermen could get by for more than a year with the same spool of line. Suit yourself. (World-record holder Walter Maxwell fished for big sharks with fresh line, but now he fishes for flounder with line that looks like it has been on his reel for five years.) But strength is not the only consideration with old line. Line does pick up scents from lubricants, sun screens, and human sweat. Tournament fishermen don't want scent tracks on their line, especially when big money is at stake.

Remember that very light line may blow all over the ocean if it's windy, while the heavier the line the fewer bites you will get. Everything from spot and flounder to big kings can be taken on 14-pound test line, so use that as a starting point. Go heavier if you fish for kings consistently, much heavier if you troll big metal lures or plugs, but a lot lighter if you will be fishing only for spot, croaker, small blues and trout.

Those two-hook heavy monofilament rigs that allow you to adjust sinkers and hooks to the fish are perfect for most beginners and handy for experienced fishermen. No more than an ounce or two of lead is necessary for most pier and surf fishing as well as small boat and inlet angling. Buy a pack of Eagle Claw hooks at the bait shop to fit what they say is biting. Buy yourself a hookstone to put an extra fine point on hooks, whether for bait or lures.

A pair of stainless steel pliers is the essential tool for all fishermen, and a fillet knife is the next most useful tool. (I have yet to find a pair of pliers that will keep its cutting edge for both wire and monofilament for more than a year; good knives are easier to find.) There is still no need of a tackle box if you can scavenge a bucket to hold pliers, knife, sinkers, and a few lures hanging inside the bucket from the rim. A few plastic boxes of hooks will fit in your pocket. But if you keep fishing, eventually you will end up as the owner of one or more tackle boxes.

What about lures? Years ago it was said that if we had but one lure to take fishing it should be a bucktail. Not true anymore. I would take a white Mann's "Swimmin' Grub" with a quarter-ounce lead-hed jig, on condition that I could have a few extra "tails" in case toothy snapper blues were biting the tails off. A few grubs in white and green or smoke are a good start, for one can catch trout, spottail, and even flounder on them. The next most useful lure is a small Floreo, a jig head with artificial hair. Fluorescent red with a white tail, it catches blues without succumbing to their teeth—blues will bite off the tails of your grubs, if not on the first fish, certainly after a few—and works on peanut (under four pounds) dolphin, trout, spottail and even flounder. My third choice is a variety of small Hopkins jigs which will take fish off the bottom close to shore or from the pier.

As for leaders, your monofilament line will do just fine, most of the time. Unless your lure spins, a snap swivel is *not* essential. A swivel does act as a short leader and may give your lure more action, but there is that much more hardware in the water to put the fish off. If blues are your main target, a short wire leader may be used. Mike Gallagher, a Myrtle Beach restaurateur, and I have filled a cooler with snapper blues taken on grubs with no wire leaders used. We lost very few of the one pounders: the trade-off is more strikes without wire leaders, but with bigger fish you will lose a lot more lures. The heavy monofilament on the two-hook bottom rigs mentioned above will also work with most fish except really big bluefish.

If you fish for spotted sea trout, get yourself a yellow or red Mirrolure—the 60M size is my favorite—but ask around among local fishermen. It works on blues, too, but with all those trebles it is not as good as a lure with just one hook such as the Floreo. Lem Winesett of Hilton Head Island swears by Mirrolures he has spray painted lime green or glowing orange. Fish it slow and deep with an occasional flip of your wrist. A white firetail grub is preferred by Neal Lewis, Morehead City's genial chamber of commerce director, when he fishes for speckled trout. For grub colors, I prefer white over inshore reefs, smoke for the ocean just outside the inlet and next to the rock jetties, and the more visible green inside the inlets.

Once you begin to acquire lures and other hardware, get a small tackle box (Plano is a good brand) and keep it clean: Throw away rusty hooks, discard unused lures or at least store them so they don't fall out when all you want is that old reliable grub, jig, or plug. Don't try to bring tackle for every possibility with you on every trip. Some anglers keep one tackle box for trout, one for flounder, and another for kings. That, of course, is the ideal that I myself set but never quite measure up to.

For years I survived with a little shoulder bag and a stringer for saltwater trout fishing. When I bought a boat and could carry more tackle, I did, but traveling light is still good advice. The same principle applies to fishing. The less terminal tackle, the simpler the rig, the sharper the hook, the neater the knots, the better the odds of catching fish. Less is more, often enough, whether in architecture or fishing for flounder, trout, and even king mackerel.

25

Casting Your Net into the Sea

Perhaps there should be a proverb about not living on borrowed mullet (or menhaden or silversides or whatever). For that is what I did for years, perhaps somewhat in awe of the semi-professional net throwers of the Carolina coast. They stand calmly in the bow of their boats or knee deep in surf or swash, line coiled in their left hand, net grasped firmly in the middle, and the hem of the net's garment firmly in their lips ("in your teeth" may send someone to the dentist for repairs if something gets caught). The leading edge of the net held in an extended right hand, the caster peers intently for the mullet either breaking the surface or sending up a slight undulation of the surface that the experienced bait hunter will respond to. Often that hunch leads to a net full of large mullet, one or two pounders not being exceptional.

As in golf, form is everything: the secret of a good shot or net throw is a smooth shoulder turn from a coiled waist and good extension. (I rarely break 90 which is why I prefer fishing to golf.) The nets, with diameters from 4 to 10 feet, are circular with lead weights at the perimeter. Draw strings are taken up after the net sinks, trapping a few dozen mullet if your aim is good, your form excellent, or your throw lucky, and the baitfish there. Beginners' luck and an abundance of baitfish help: On my first throw with a five-foot net I took some 30 finger mullet and with my first throw with a seven-footer I landed about 10 pounds of "biguns," the kind of mullet that split and broiled fresh make a tasty meal for a hungry man, a meal that no true gourmet, that is one with an open mind, could resist. But like the great flycast that does not draw a strike, a fully open net against a blue sky is its own reward—at least until you get tired of throwing the net and not catching any bait. In good weather, from spring through early fall, it's hard not to catch something in your net in any coastal Carolina or Georgia creek from half tide down past the turn.

Live mullet are rarely sold at baitshops, even dockside or creekside operations, and there are times when a fat mud minnow, bought from the baitman, is not the best bait for flounder, spottail, or trout. The other reason you will want to invest $30 or more in a good net—I recommend monofilament, for it sinks fast, rather than linen, but watch the oyster shells that can tear a net up—is that there is so much live bait available to catch with a net that the net will pay for itself in a season.

Besides mullet, you can catch shrimp for bait or for table (but do check your state's regulations), small squid (an ideal bait for inshore bottomfishing trips), spearing or white bait, which make good trout bait or which can be fried whole as in the "white bait" delicacy of the coasts of Europe, and a tremendous variety of other species that our Southeast coastal marshes have as nursery guests. (Two days after I wrote the first draft of this chapter,

A cast net provides both bait and food for coastal anglers.

Seining for shrimp in a South Carolina creek, two recreational anglers are watched by a commercial fisherman who was transplanting oysters.

Lloyd Burroughs and I caught a one-pound flounder, dozens of mullet, a number of houndfish and halfbeaks—close relatives of the ballyhoo, miniature billfish and great bait—in the course of a few net flings at Huntington Beach State Park south of Murrells Inlet, South Carolina.)

Every grade school science teacher should learn to throw a net just to show those wise-guy fourth graders on that next trip to the beach that teacher can do something besides stand in front of the class. Of course, some practice beforehand is essential. The dedicated angler's kind of tackle shop (you'll know it when you see it, or at least as soon as you walk in the door, certainly not at K-Mart) usually has someone there who can give you a quick primer on how to cast your net.

There is a whole school of net throwers who never hold the net in their lips or teeth. They don't know the joys of tasting the mudflats nor the exciting grit of sand on their tongues. They are probably laughing at me now, as I did at a companion who asked me where the three-pound bluefish came from that was jumping around in the bottom of my boat with some mullet I had just netted. Casting your net in our coastal waters can be its own reward.

Pulling a Seine Net

One haul with a seine net in a Southeast coastal marsh in August should convince anyone but the most greedy "developer" of the importance of our wetlands.

Pick a coastal marsh, any coastal marsh, from the barrier islands of the Georgia and South Carolina coast up to Bald Head Island, North Carolina, and beyond. Take a youngster, any youngster, from four or five on up to the age when the sense of wonder disappears. Your grandmother may even qualify, if she doesn't mind getting her tennis sneakers muddy. But a young boy or girl or two are the ideal companions to help to pull a seine net for bait and profit.

The profit is in seeing what our coastal marshes have to offer: mud minnows, mullet, flounder of many kinds, from an inch long to, if you're lucky, a few pounds—I saw a five pounder seined at Cherry Grove near Little River Inlet one late summer's day. There are also squid in mid summer, shrimp, silversides, juvenile croaker, spot, pompano, bluefish, toadfish, sea robins, and many other fishes. Blueclaw crabs in various sizes click their claws at you; you'll sometimes find a pair of big blueclaws, one of them a softshell, plus a variety of other crabs from hermits to rock and spider crabs. A large eel may even give you a surprise as it splashes snakelike in your net. Use a towel to grab it if you want a good dinner, or just watch it find its own way back to the water from the mud, sand, or shell bank where you empty your net.

Check state regulations on net size. (In South Carolina, for example, mesh openings that are legal for seining minnows are not legal for seining shrimp.) Generally, the local tackle shop can tell you. Experience, patience, persistence, and luck determine the catch. The last two hours of the outgoing tide are best. At high water it is difficult to catch anything in the creeks, but in the shallow waters next to a jetty you might still make a good haul of baitfish.

Move slowly, keeping the net spread wide and the poles pointed at a 45-degree angle to the bottom. Make a wide circle and come up on a spot of shore that is neither too muddy nor too covered with sharp oyster shells. As you pull against what remains of the tide you may see shrimp and mullet leaping over your net, but pay them no mind. Enough will stay in to make the last few yards a crescendo of fish life flipping as you ease the net out of the water. Take what you can use for bait or aquarium or table, and let the rest swim free. By now an egret or two may have edged closer, and if you are on an inlet beach near the ocean, terns or gulls may be hovering overhead, and herons may stand watching just a few yards away, their appetites whetted by your wholesale harvest and their own chances of cleaning the bank of your leftovers after you move back into the creek. Leave a bait bucket uncovered and the birds may help themselves.

We keep a cooler and a few buckets handy for bait and possible dinners. In the summer, a single haul in a South Carolina inlet may produce a pound or more of shrimp, a few blueclaws, and assorted other fishes. Mullet are not as hardy as mud minnows, but both should be placed in a bucket that allows the creek water to circulate. Fish to be saved for cut bait should be placed on the ice promptly.

The marine life captured in a few passes with a seine net may convince you that a saltwater aquarium would be a rewarding educational investment for you and your children. But I know how costly and time consuming one can be, so my children and I simply commit to memory the results of each draw. The juvenile gamefish—flounder, of course, but even baby pompano and grouper—are evidence of the nursery service our Southeast coastal marshlands provide for the whole Atlantic coast. We also catch a lot of bait and an occasional delicious softshell crab appetizer. If you get lucky, you may even feel the thud of a flounder or spottail bass hitting your billowing seine and flopping out on the mud with the rest of your catch, instant dinner and a tribute to what our marsh creeks mean to sportfishing. As long as our coastal marshes are clean, seining will be fun and rewarding.

Seining and Live-Bait Notes: Store your net in a dry place after allowing it to dry in the sun. With occasional repairs, a good net can last for five years or more. Long-sleeved shirts, long pants, and sneakers are a good idea to protect against foot cuts, biting flies, sunburn, and jellyfish stings, all of which are possible in the marsh. More often than not, however, just the sneakers and shorts will do. Take a youngster or two seining for bait soon. Even if the big ones aren't biting, you can still say you caught a bunch.

Small mullet ("finger" mullet) or mud minnows (also known as killies or mummichubs elsewhere on the coast) are easily kept alive in a plastic trolling bucket that allows the water to flow through it. Hang it over the side as you slow your boat to troll; pull it up when you're moving fast or you'll get splashed. Change the water every five minutes in hot weather while you're moving from place to place: R.D. Brigham refers to this as giving the mullet "a bath." Fresh, oxygen-rich water is essential for the mullet; mud minnows are tougher and will often survive over-night even if the water is not changed. For larger mullet use an on-board live-bait well with water circulated by a battery-powered aerator or use a cooler and keep changing the water.

Mullet and mud minnows fished for flounder, drum, and trout are best hooked through the lips. Treat your bait gently and you'll catch more dinners. When fished on the bottom with a sliding-sinker rig mullet may also be hooked just in front of the tail. Captain Mike Conner of Georgetown Landing Marina on Winyah Bay points out that sun screens and insect repellents should be washed from your hands before handling a baitfish because the sense of smell is so acute for most fish. He notes that even old line can take on the scent of lubricating oil or human sweat, so bait should also be free of what to the fish are unnatural smells.

26

Fishing for Bait

My boat was anchored some 20 yards from a favorite trout hole that lay just a few feet from the edge of the marsh. Two speckled trout of a few pounds each gave an occasional but weakening thump from the cooler. As I cast a spray-painted-at-home orange Mirrolure plug toward the bank, the sound of a larger engine invaded the quiet of the late afternoon. Would I have to share my favorite trout hole? The prospect was like a thunderhead at eleven in the morning on a beach picnic day, a threat to ruin everything that was best in this early autumn excursion. Fortunately, the intruder was just searching for bait.

For him catching live bait was the difference between having a shot at winning a big money king mackerel and trusting to luck. The menhaden might be off the beaches the next day for those who could find them and throw a net the size of a parachute, but this angler was determined to put some pinfish in his live-bait tank just for insurance. (The pinfish, shaped like a bream, is extremely hardy, an excellent baitfish for float fishing or even for drift fishing for kings. Even when hooked in the back, a pinfish will swim all day if treated kindly otherwise.)

He anchored his boat and fished with sinker, small hooks, and bits of cut bait, occasionally putting a three- to four-ounce pinfish in his live-bait tank. It was an insurance policy for the next day's fishing. Other fishes are worth catching for live bait: small bluefish, in fact, are among the best live baits for trolling, drifting, or float fishing. Offshore a bit, the sailors choice, which is a member of the grunt family, makes a fine live bait, and out toward the snapper banks the tomtate, another grunt, is an effective live bait.

Not only king mackerel and cobia, but tarpon, big bluefish, sharks, and even spottail bass may be caught by "trading up" from small baitfish taken on light tackle and then used as live bait. The fact is that there is an alternative to "fish or cut bait," and that is fishing for small baitfish to be used for big gamefish. On any offshore trip, it pays to have a light rod with 20-pound test line, small hooks, and six ounces of lead to use to catch live bait from the bottom. (On occasion, these small hook rigs have captured specimens not previously identified as being taken north of Florida; an example would be a lovely green, blue, and yellow fish, a yellow wrasse that I later presented, frozen, to marine scientist Dr. Richard Moore at Coastal Carolina College.)

My favorite "trade-up" story involves a Georgia boy named Charley Johnson. After a few decades of production work with the *Augusta Chronicle*, he decided to get some more golfing and fishing time by moving to the beach. It turned out that when I first took him fishing for bream on the Waccamaw River, he was fishing the same river his father, Charles Putney Johnson, fished when he was a lad before moving to Georgia. Anyway, after a trip on the river I suggested to Charley that we try for flounder at Murrells Inlet.

It was one of those sweet late May days, when the water is clear, the ocean calm, and the sun shining brightly. J.B. Orr, who was then co-proprietor of Inlet Port Marina, was kind enough to tell us that some nice catches of flatfish had been made drifting mud minnows right in the mouth of the inlet. Off we went, cutting a path through the back creeks, and soaking up the sheer perfection of a fishing morning full of promise. When I am in such a mood because of nature's kindness I often find that the fish I seek are in a good mood, that is, feeding eagerly. So it was with the flounder, as we took one or two on each drift on the incoming tide.

Charley had another bite, but this one ran with the bait and came splashing to the surface. It was a bluefish, a bit under a pound, and I netted it with more than usual care. "Nice fish, Charley," I said and he smiled, proud of his first blue. His smile changed to a puzzled expression as I slid a hook attached to a wire leader with a trailing treble into the blue's lips. "What are you doing with my fish, Don?" I thought Charley was being a bit too possessive for a share-and-share fishing trip, but I didn't want to be critical of my guest. "Let's see if we can get a king to hit," I commented and let out some line on a heavier rod that I had brought along for just this situation. Twenty-five-pound-test line, a Penn Jigmaster reel, a wire leader with a trailing treble hanging about three-quarters down the side of that still frisky blue—I put the outfit in a rod holder and went back to flounder fishing.

Charley was sure I was going to lose his beautiful bluefish to a shark. His fears were reasonable, but my hopes were for a king mackerel, and we both had our suspicions aroused by a sudden fast and persistent clicking of the reel. "You got a shark, Don" was Charley's mournful and reproachful comment. After the fish had run off line for a minute or so it finally came to a halt and the line went slack. Now it was running at an angle toward us but it was still hooked. Charley waited to see my shark and his direful predictions confirmed.

The silvery torpedo shape that glided toward the boat was just what I had hoped for. Just before it surged away from the boat, I tried to sound casual as I asked my guest if he had ever gaffed a king. He reckoned that he could learn, and after a few minutes more of give and take with the line, I moved the fish within an arm's length of my companion who set the gaff as neatly as Captain Don Lash in his best gaffing form. On the scales, the king would go 22 pounds. For the moment, it barely fit the big cooler that occupied the middle of my little aluminum boat.

I resisted the temptation to say "I told you so," but my grin gave me away and we both laughed about the "shark." Still, Charley would not admit that the king was worth his bluefish. His ensuing conduct, however, more than made up for his tempo-rary lack of trust in his guide and his reluctance in donating his baitfish for a greater cause. As so often happens, the wind picked up at noon and the tide changed, forcing us out of the mouth of the inlet. We went a bit offshore and resumed bottomfishing, letting out a drift line with another live bluefish on for kings.

A small boat went by, apparently slow trolling for kings, and the skipper yelled over to ask us what we had caught. We answered with the truth, a few flounder and a king. "How big a king?" We reckoned that it might go 15 pounds, but there was something in the tone of his "let's see it" response that may have annoyed even as easy-going a humanitarian as my companion. No one could have rubbed it in more dramatically as Charley reached into the cooler and slowly raised the king all the way out so the obviously doubting Captain Thomas could see that we weren't kidding.

"What did you catch him on?" The fine edge of unbelief was gone from the fisherman's voice, but I felt he had to do a little penance for his lack of faith in our veracity. "Stingray grub," I called back, and to Charley's credit he, too, kept a straight face.

So sometimes we fish to catch bait, a spot for a spottail bass, a whiting for a flounder, a pinfish for a king, an eel for a cobia, even a peanut dolphin for a big blue marlin. But good old Charley Johnson's first bluefish will probably be my best trade-up ever. He won't let me forget it, either.

27

Bad Days

There are perfectly miserable fishing days, but barring accidents, they should not be a total loss. Usually, one gets involved with rain, too much wind, and cold temperatures not out of foolishness but from friendship. For example, good old Mitch Godwin wants to take his son fishing and you promise to pick them up before dawn on an autumn Saturday.

The night before may have been starlit with just a little breeze, but the last hours of night bring forth northeasterly winds that seem to have doubled in intensity by the time we reach the launching ramp. Still, the fisherman is not always content until he actually looks at the ocean. Curiosity drives on more than cats or how many times have we had a hurricane off the Florida coast and the king mackerel were tearing up everything trolled past them offshore?

So despite the flags flapping hard and the occasional snap of ropes against flagpoles, we set off for the mouth of the inlet, noticing that the water in the creek is exceptionally high. Dawn has not brought sunshine, but at least it's not raining. We live and go fishing always in hope.

There is too much surf even inside the inlet to beach the boat except in a lagoon and the wind even blows us off the lee shore there. Flocks of skimmers and gulls have claimed their own segregated sections of the beach and my friend's son, Sean, is kind enough to chuckle at my comment on birds of a feather. Perhaps because the wind and waves have forced the baitfish into the creek, there are mullet to be caught with the net on almost every cast. Just the week before (I recall this to reassure myself in the face of the wretched day) with Hurricane Gloria bearing down on the Carolinas and the Arthur Smith King Mackerel Tournament cancelled, a boatload of anglers still managed three kings, one a 29 pounder, in the mouth of the inlet. Today there is no hurricane approaching, but the northeast winds continue strong, despite our hopes. A more impartial observer might note that they are blowing harder and that rain is imminent, too.

I pull on my slicker top and put on a pair of Goretex pants I use on the golf course. Mitch and Sean struggle into their ponchos. We head out of the lagoon for the mouth of the inlet, but before we have traveled 50 yards spray is coming over the bow. Even between the two protecting arms of the jetties the boat makes way slowly against the wind. But the temperature is in the 70's so we can tolerate a bit of water.

Why did the disciples take one more cast of their nets, even though they had fished all night and caught nothing? Was it just their faith and the commanding voice of their friend on shore? Probably so, but both faith and trust in that biblical scene were perhaps based on the natural sense of hope in the fisherman whether it is for one last productive cast or that the weather will begin to improve. Despite overwhelming contraindications, I nurture a glimmer of hope of sneaking past the jetties and fishing in the lee of the south jetties. The tide is starting to flow strong. Charter boats have already come back in, one later reporting to me the sight of kings skyrocketing in the mouth of the inlet. One king will save the day, but there is a cloud on the horizon—actually a few of them. If we get into the sheltered water will we sit there being soaked by the rain as the waves build up in the mouth of the inlet as tide runs against wind?

It is unfair to burden your guests with choices on a rotten day. I head the boat back in and despite the wind I think I detect a sigh of relief from Mitch, hunched as he is in the bow. In the first creek mouth we find anglers anchored and fishing for trout.

181

Johnny McDowell is working a grub from his 14-foot boat but he shakes his head sadly. I remember seeing him come in from spending eight hours of a raw November day fishing for trout from his small boat—it was during a Shriners benefit, a trout tournament—and I thought at the time that a lesser man might have died of exposure. He looked like a man who had suffered, but unless he fishes only in beautiful weather, every fisherman knows the experience.

A big blue heron makes his awkward leap into the leaden sky and goes lumbering off over the lush spartina grass as we anchor in the "Brigham Hole" where 35 years ago R.D. Brigham noticed an old black man "forking" flounder, probing the bottom with a pitchfork and slowly filling an old cooler with fresh forked flounder. Today we will use rod, reel, and our king mackerel baits, the smaller mullet, to fish for flounder. The rain finally comes down in intermittent screens driven by the wind. The fish are not biting. Let's cut our losses. We head back through sheets of rain toward the marina, hoping that nothing goes wrong with the motor. If the temperature were only 20 degrees lower it would be brutal, if not dangerous, to be out on the water.

Cutting one's losses on such a day is the only way. Still, we did look at the ocean, we did assure ourselves that nothing would be caught, and we did cure ourselves of fishing fever—at least until the next fair day beckoned us back with clear skies and gentle breezes. These, more than any sense of testing oneself against the elements, are the virtues salvageable from a bad day of fishing.

We could resolve to go fishing only if the weather were nearly perfect, but then we would miss those occasional days when the seas are unfit for fishermen but there is a bit of shelter behind the rocks or in the creeks and the spottail, blues, or trout are biting. The March days when Nelson Bryant stopped by on his way back up north from Florida and we tagged and released an eight-pound red drum while the seas smashed the other side of the rocks; the November day my then 10-year-old Sara and her friend, Michael Tolley, and I cleaned our abundant catch of snapper blues as pelicans swam around us and the north winds stirred up even the inlet creek where we anchored; the day a construction worker and I carried a stringer of two- to four-pound winter trout away from the beach at Pawleys Island in the wind and rain . . . those were the bad days that we turned to good.

As recompense for those "bad days" on the water, there is the occasional perfect combination of weather, water, and fish.

Every experienced fisherman on our Southeast coast has similar experiences and memories. And every fisherman lives in hope, until he has to cut his losses. Bad days are learning experiences, too.

28

Fishless Days

Not catching fish is bad if you fish for a living or to feed your family. It also hurts, to a much lesser degree, if you have wagered heavily on your fish-catching prowess—the entry fee to a big king mackerel tournament or buying yourself in the Calcutta or betting pool of a billfish tournament. The true sport fisherman, however—the angler who never sells his catch but fishes for the sheer enjoyment of the sport, not excluding the delights of fresh seafood on his table—knows that fishless days can be quite profitable.

Bad weather aside, those days when the fish just won't bite are a reminder that no matter how fine our tackle, long our experience, and persistent our efforts, if the fish don't want to bite they won't. We can use our skill to present seductive baits, try another technique, even slap the water with a rod to fool some fish into a feeding frenzy, or put out a slick of ground bunker chum to encourage them. But some days they just won't bite. Period.

Just being out on the water is one justification for these days. The fog rolled in yesterday—or I should say—rolled off the beach and left me in a circle of flat ocean: no birds, no other boats, and nothing going after my drifting live mullet. A small shark hit a piece of cut mullet I was fishing on bottom in hopes of catching a small blue for live bait. Only the set of the sea, the direction of the breeze which had come off the land (of course, it could have changed), a glimmer of sunshine, and the sound of the surf served as directional guides as I made my way back to shore.

Even with big fresh mullet that I had just caught in my throw net, I could not get a king to strike. A school of jack crevalle smashed into baitfish around the mouth of the inlet, but my heart was set on a king and none was forthcoming. A flock of pelicans cruised slowly along the ocean just off the beach. I cruised after them and headed back into the inlet. Was the day a loss? Of course not.

Fresh air, warming sunshine after the fog rolled away, the memory of the solitude of the fog-enshrouded ocean and the jacks leaping in the morning air, the mobile geometry of the flight of those pelicans, all made the morning superior to any but the best of churchly sermons.

But any avid fisherman knows and the novice will soon discover that there is another benefit of a fishless day: It cures you of the habit, at least for a while. "The inshore king mackerel (or trout or bluefish or shad or flounder) are through for the year," you can now tell yourself, but you have experienced it as well. It is easier to clean boat and tackle and get back to spend some more time with your family, building up those credits that can be cashed in as the next phase of our Southeast coast fishing begins.

An angler goes home after a day of fishing from a jetty.
Even when no fish are caught, a day on the water can be
its own reward.

Appendix

Suggested Reading

Goldstein, Robert J., *Pier Fishing in North Carolina*, (Winston-Salem, John F. Blair, 1978)

Hoese, H. Dixon, and Moore, Richard, *Fishes of the Gulf of Mexico*, (College Station, Texas A & M Press, 1977)

Millus, Donald, *A Contemplative Fishing Guide to the Grand Strand*, (Lexington, The Sandlapper Store, Inc., 1977)

Poucher, Dean J., *A Guide to Fishing Hilton Head Island*, (Hilton Head Island, Island Typo Graphics, 1983)

Reiger, George, *Wanderer on My Native Shore*, (New York, Simon and Schuster, 1983)

State Information Sources

(These are excellent sources for free maps, as well as lists of headboats, charter boats, piers, and marinas. Tell them where you plan to fish, and they can be very helpful.)

Georgia: Coastal Resources Division, Department of Natural Resources, 1200 Glynn Avenue, Brunswick, Ga. 31523

North Carolina: North Carolina Department of Commerce, 430 North Salisbury Street, Raleigh, N.C. 27611

South Carolina: South Carolina Wildlife and Marine Resources Department, P.O. Box 12559, Charleston, S.C. 29412

N.B. The *Angler's Guide to the United States Atlantic Coast, Section VI,* False Cape, Virginia, to Altamaha Sound, Georgia, contains good fishing maps (not for navigation) and much useful local information. It is available from the Superintendent of Documents, U.S. Government Printing Office, Washington, D.C. 20402. Stock No. 003-020-00097.

Tags

If you wish to contribute to the future of the sport, why not tag and release a fish or two your next time out? The following sources provide tags free or at cost. Write for further information.

American Littoral Society
Sandy Hook, N.J. 07732

National Marine Fisheries Service
Narragansett Laboratory
South Ferry Road
Narragansett, R.I. 02992-1191

North Carolina Division of Marine Fisheries
Marine Resources Department
P.O. Box 769
Morehead City, N.C. 28557

South Carolina Wildlife and Marine Resources Department
P.O. Box 12559
Charleston, S.C. 29412

INDEX

INDEX

INDEX